My Story
by *Marilyn Chambers*

"When I named the faces on The Female Mt. Rushmore of XXX last year... the first was Marilyn Chambers, followed by Seka, Ginger Lynn, and Jenna Jameson. (For the record... the The Male Mt. Rushmore of XXX includes Harry Reems, John C. Holmes, Jamie Gillis, and Ron Jeremy.)"

– Bill Margold

"When I first started in the business in the late '70s, Marilyn Chambers was an inspiration. She was the epitome of glamour, fame and success! You can't imagine what a thrill it was to work with Marilyn and then direct her later adult projects. But more than anything I treasured our friendship—as women, mothers and as actresses. She was always a very class act."

– Veronica Hart

"Like John Holmes was amongst the men, Marilyn Chambers was with the women. The two of them were in a class all by themselves, the King and Queen of the Golden Age of Porn. I was lucky enough to work with Marilyn three times, but it was only after Chuck Traynor was gone during that third and final time, that I finally got a delightful glimpse at the real woman behind the mask of the Ivory Snow femme fatale—and she was warm and wonderful. I will treasure those memories always."

– Howie Gordon (aka Richard Pacheco)

"I knew Marilyn, worked with her in both her film *Insatiable* and at the O'Farrell Theatre in San Francisco. She was a huge star and I was in awe of her, but she was very kind to me. Putting me at ease, she got me very hot and bothered with her sex play. We had lots of fun together! She was foxy, lean and clean. Her sexual enthusiasm created great stirrings in other's libidos!"

– Serena

My Story

by *Marilyn Chambers*

Written by the girl next door who became the world's most famous Adult Film Star during the Sexual Revolution, paving the way for so many others to follow her footsteps into the World of Porn.

Foreword by McKenna Taylor

BearManor Media

2014

My Story by Marilyn Chambers

© 1975 & 2014 by the Estate of Marilyn Chambers

For information, address:

Valerie Gobos
Gobos Film & Entertainment, Inc.
1000 N. Kingsbury, #102
Chicago, Illinois 60610
P: 312-836-8300
E: val@gobosinc.com
www.valeriegobos.com

or

BearManor Media
P. O. Box 71426
Albany, GA 31708
bearmanormedia.com

Typesetting by John Teehan

Published in the USA by BearManor Media

ISBN— 1-59393-439-4
978-1-59393-439-2

Foreword
by McKenna Taylor

My mother was Marilyn Taylor, the most loving and understanding woman I've ever known. My mother was special, she had an air about her that was unmatched by anyone I've known to this day. I did not know the women who wrote this book and started the legacy of Marilyn Chambers but I am extremely proud of her. When writing this book, I believe my mother  wanted people to know who the girl next door and behind that green door really was. To me she's just my mom.

My mother taught me many important lessons and at the top of that list was honesty. She never lied to me. I remember finding out who my mother was, along with many of my friends at the time, no doubt recognized by their parents. She was willing to tell me everything once I was ready to know, which I wasn't for a big chunk of my life. When I was ready to hear about her life "adventures" we sat down, and she let me lead the conversation. We had a wonderful open talk, with lots of gasps and laughs. I asked her every question you could imagine, and she gave me nothing but the truth in her responses.

My mother was a phenomenal chef, and I'm not just saying that because I am her daughter. She would always be in the kitchen creating new recipes for my friends and I to try. Besides cooking my mother loved being outside, gardening and taking our dogs for walks. Friendship was big for my mother because when she called you her friend, that is what you were. She would do anything for you and was extremely loyal.

There is no doubt that my mother had an exciting life with experiences left and right. Whenever I needed anything I knew I could come to her and never had to be afraid or embarrassed. Even my closest friends would talk to her about things they couldn't open up about to their own parents.

Knowing my mother had such a monumental impact upon the sexual revolution takes my breath away. Every decision she made not only impacted her but the world in its entirety. When my mom was in her prime of the adult film industry, she explained it to me as a glamorous and exciting lifestyle. She got to see a different side of the world and that industry that most never will. She was able to express herself and her sexuality in the time period where it was just becoming acceptable to do so.

Even though my mother accomplished many things by such a young age she also expressed the darker side of things. She wanted to break out into mainstream media, which she honestly thought was possible. Unfortunately her career outside of the adult film industry was minimal. My mother was in no way shape or form ashamed of the work she had done. She had fun and it was the 70s! She grew up and matured fast which I'm so very proud of her for. She really was an amazing actress and talented in so many different ways. My mother could be having the worst day, sweating her butt off, but if someone wanted to take her picture, she'd flash that sexy smile that we all know she had down perfectly. If she was busy or making dinner and the phone rang for a radio interview, she'd put the dog in her lap, clear her throat and give the best damn interview anyone ever could. When I saw my mom incorporate two different lives, the life of Marilyn Chambers and the life of an amazing mother it amazed me. She was courageous and strong in everything that was thrown her way.

My mother had no regrets but she did tell me that if I made any move toward that industry she'd kick my butt.

She was extremely protective of me and wanted to give me the best life she could offer, which she did without saying.

My mother is and always will be a legend.

After she opened that "green door" she showed people a world full of sexual expression and freedom that many people were too afraid to do on their own. I thank Marilyn Chambers for all that she has done for not just the adult film industry, but for the confidence she has instilled in the millions of people who are now proud of their sexual freedom. I thank Marilyn Taylor for the best 17 years of my life and for being the best mother I could have ever asked for. I will try my best to make her proud for the rest of the days of my life. I love you Mommy.

1

Behind the Green Door

The day Linda Lovelace walked out of Chuck Traynor's life he walked into mine. *Walked* isn't the right word—he called. I answered. We talked. And with that phone call began the transformation into what I am today, the Marilyn Chambers you know. I want this book to tell you everything about my life and my thoughts, especially about the Marilyn Chambers you don't know.

Yes, I was Marilyn Chambers at the time Chuck Traynor called me with the offer of becoming my personal manager, but I wasn't the person who's writing this book today. Sure, I was known. My face was on every box of Ivory Snow in every supermarket in the country, the 99 & 44/100% pure young mother. In every major city in the country (and some minor ones, wherever the local law would allow) for five dollars you could see me sucking a big black cock in *Behind the Green Door*, and squealing, "Fuck me, Frank. Fuck me hard!" in *The Resurrection of Eve. Green Door* stills of torso—black evening gown, pearls around the neck, the Ivory Snow pose with a taste of sex—traveled around on top of taxi cabs in Los Angeles and peered down over the throngs in New York's Times Square from a gigantic billboard. Marilyn Chambers, porno star and Ivory Soap girl, rah rah rah!

At the time all that was going on I was still very much Marilyn Briggs, a happily married and very devoted housewife in Walnut Creek, California. You saw me vacuum a rug in *The Resurrection of Eve*? It was an easy scene to play. I actually did that when I got home from shooting! Doug and I were nearly a typical young suburban couple, the exception being that it was me who went out and did the work (yes, work is work, even if that work is all about pleasure, such as jerking off two big cocks attached to two hunky men swinging above you on a trapeze) and Doug stayed home and wondered what he was going to do with his life. I was content, or so I made myself believe. I say that because underneath my housewife facade lay the most basic desire of my life, one I'd had since my days in grade school in Connecticut—to make it as an actress and entertainer.

And Chuck Traynor, in his phone call and the many others that were to follow, gave me the chance to become just what I'd dreamed of. It was suddenly all real, right there. I knew it would take hard work, but at least it was finally reachable. You could stick your arm out and grab it and if you held on long enough....

Stardom. And what's that all about? I'm not sure, but maybe I will be by the time I'm finished writing this. I do know one thing: I love it. I love being known as a sex symbol, I love to hear people tell me they'd like to ball me. I think it's terrific when a guy tells me he thinks I'm a great cocksucker or when a chick tells me she loves my body and would like to make love to me. Or when a gay guy tells me because he's seen my films, he learned some new ways of pleasing his lover. I find them all compliments and they are gratifying. It's a far out thing to get people to like you and desire you and it pleases me a lot. I love sex, I love doing love scenes on camera, and I always will. I never want to let go of that part of my life, my career. But I want people to know there is another side as well, the actress and singer and dancer....

And more than that, the person.

Hopefully—with Chuck's help, for my story is in many ways his story too—this book, my first attempt at writing anything more than a letter, will tell you the Marilyn Chambers story through truthful eyes.

I'll always believe that the best attribute a person can have is the ability to be honest about himself.

Criss-cross my heart!

Behind the Green Door was called "...the Rolls-Royce of porno films" in one review, and it's the film that started it all for me so I guess it's the right way to start my story.

One day in San Francisco—you'll read all about my San Francisco days later—where I was trying desperately to break into theater, I saw an ad in the paper for a big-budget commercial film. I immediately thought, Far out! That's what I've been waiting for! I mean I had visions of another *Gone With the Wind* being shot in San Francisco and I was high with enthusiasm and hope when I walked into the office that had been listed in the ad. Funny, one day after shooting, my wind *was* nearly *gone* from all the cocksucking!

I had never guessed it was going to be a porno film, so I got a little uptight when I realized it. I mean when you're given a questionnaire which asks *Will you perform hard-core sex on screen?*, anyone with half a brain knows what kind of film it's going to be. So I said no. Any sexual experience I'd had had been private—I didn't think I would be *able* to fuck on camera; I thought I'd break out in a rash and go crazy or something.

So I met the Mitchell brothers even though I had said I wouldn't do any fucking in the film, because there were clothed parts to be filled too. They looked me over and tried to talk me into changing my mind. Jim Mitchell said something at the time, which has been repeated by reviewers and audiences all over the country, and I'm flattered every time I hear it. He said, "Marilyn, you're the girl next door. You're not the pimple-assed chicks who suck cock on camera for a living and spend their bread on speed; you are the typical American sweetheart. You're the face every guy dreams of shoving his cock into but never does because he can't *find* you! You're fresh air and apple pie." (He was right—I do look like the WASP chick next door—I mean, if Procter & Gamble picked my face to illustrate the essence of "99 & 44/100% pure" Americana, there's a hell of a lot of truth in Jim's statement.) So fresh-air-and-apple-pie-me thought about it and called back. "I'm reconsidering," I told them, "and I want to know how badly you want me."

"Like very badly," Jim said.

"Meaning more money and a percentage?"

Jim choked and mumbled to his brother, Artie, and then said, "Yeah, we want you *that* bad."

I told them I'd think about it. Wow, I was really playing a Katherine Hepburn thing, asking for a percentage. I did it almost a joke (thinking there was no way in hell I could get it) and also because I had been burned before and this time I wanted some kind of security. I sat around for a few days, beginning to believe some other girl-next-door type had waltzed into the Mitchell brothers' office and swept them off their feet for less money and no percentage. I started to think I'd blown the whole thing just when I was kind of getting to *like* the idea of doing sex on the screen. I had a sneaky feeling that porno was going to become big stuff (not nearly as "in" and chic as it has become, but at least very acceptable as a form of entertainment, and certainly profitable) and if things happened in the right way, making a name in porno could give someone the basis for building a career. And wasn't that what I always wanted?

Well, Jim Mitchell hadn't found that other "down home" chick, and he called and offered me a lot of money and a nice percentage. I got a copy of the script from him and liked the title because it was intriguing and also because I remembered a song that Dorothy Collins used to sing on *Your Hit Parade* when I was very young, "…green door, what's that secret you're keeping?", which had always been one of my dad's favorites. So I read it and got turned on by it and said yes.

And the rest is history.

But that history is interesting. You see, when I was growing up I had a lot of sexual fantasies, as everyone does, and the best one—I think every woman has this fantasy at one time or another—was seeing myself being raped and violated and forced into submission, especially by a black man. And there it was, on paper in front of me, my whole masturbation trip ready for the screen. So I broke down those inhibitions I'd had very quickly because I knew making the film would be a good thing for me, not only career-wise but as an actress and as a person, because I would live out and turn on to a sexual dream which I'd probably never have had the chance to realize in my lifetime. What happened to me doing the film is the same thing that happens to women who see it in the theaters—they put themselves into the part of Gloria and what is being done to her is being done to them.

I also liked the fact that I had not one word to say in the entire film—talk about a submission fantasy! It was as though I were bound and gagged the entire time. Gloria checks in at a hotel in Sausalito and as she's going out for the evening, just as her date is arriving, she's abducted by strange men and driven to a private club, where she's hypnotized by a woman and then brought out onto a stage to be watched by the club's members, a very odd assortment of people. First she's fondled by several women—they caress her and kiss her and take turns eating her pussy—and then a big black stud (Johnnie Keyes, a former prizefighter and dancer) wearing white tights with the crotch cut out enters and fucks her forever. In the background is a green door, and when it is opened and Gloria is taken behind it she encounters two studs on a trapeze, their cocks hard, ready for her to beat off, while sucking off a third, as yet another guy fucks her. It's the Ringling Brothers, Barnum & Bailey act of big-time porno, a circus of sex. And while Gloria is being showered with semen, the club members have an orgy of their own.

And that's about it—all fantasy. The film is really a flashback fantasy a trucker has, which he tells in a diner. That story had been around for ages, real truckers had passed it back and forth, and the Mitchell brothers heard it and turned it into a movie. The story is simplicity itself. Like

I said, I don't say a word—which was probably harder to act because I had to convey any emotion with my eyes and lips (if something wasn't stuck *in* my lips at the time!). It's a good film, a very good film. I look at it today and think it could have been better only because it was filmed in the midst of chaos because the Mitchell brothers were in court over another film. It was filmed too quickly. But what's done is done, and audiences seem to love it, and that's what counts.

People always ask me how the end of *Behind the Green Door* was shot, the artistic few minutes at the end of the picture where the screen is filled with color as many different cocks shoot all over my face. The process is called polarization and is shot is slow motion, or really stop-action. Click click click. Come come come. Color is put in afterward and that's how they arrive at the bright reds and greens and make the image look like a negative. It's a hard process, and expensive too, but it's worth it—most people I've talked to say that that segment is the biggest turn-on they've ever seen.

What was it like, filming that sequence, filming those come scenes? Well, I'll tell you. About five or six different guys were used, for starters. We shot a lot of footage on that because those come scenes, which were to be strung together later as one *looooooooog* come scene, were the "feel" of the picture audiences would take home with them, because the sequence would be the end of the film and unlike anything in it till that point. I think that's why critics dug the film a whole lot, because that scene broke out of the old porno mold of hand-held cameras and lousy color and showed people that there's a great deal of beauty in the mystery and majesty of an orgasm. I call it artsy-fartsy now because I've seen it so many times but the first time a person views it they're kind of knocked out by it, kind of stunned. They say, "Wow! That's really beautiful!" And they get all horny inside.

And, of course, that sequence is the ultimate in the fantasy of man conquering woman. What's a better turn-on than five different guys jerking off all over a pretty girl's face and letting her lick their sperm from her lips and chin?

It was exhausting work, that's for sure. I can dig the value of it now, the fantasy it portrayed, but I felt humiliated doing it. And that was the point, I know, that Gloria be humiliated as guy after guy explodes onto her face, but I felt humiliated myself, as an actress and a person, to have to get into a back-breaking position (so the camera angle would be just right) and stay there while one guy after another worked his cock over my face … and I'd have to stare up at it, hoping it would shoot fast because my knees were killing me and my neck felt ready for a brace … and when he finally shot off I had to devour his jism and nearly swim in it, only to have him replaced by another … and the position seemed worse, painful … humiliating. That's why the sequence seems so real—it was! It's exciting because it's honest.

I couldn't foresee how it would look on screen, being in that contorted position, being filmed with three different cameras from three different angles. It took about five hours all together. One guy couldn't get it up and we sat around waiting (my only rest!) until he yelled, "I got it!" and I had to rush into position before it softened. I felt like a baseball player sliding to second base. It was a mad rush because we didn't have time to waste and we needed to catch his orgasm on camera. It would have been wonderful to do it with just one guy, but after two orgasms, there's no jism left to spurt, and that's why we used so many different guys—the cream had to *pour* out of their cocks, which, again, is a great fantasy.

That orgasm—the guy who yelled, "I got it!"—was the one that dribbled into my mouth, if you remember from the film. I've been asked, "Why didn't you swallow it?" The answer to that is, first off, I wasn't exactly spitting it out, you know? I mean, for God's sake, I was blowing bubbles with it and gurgling it in my throat and letting it run over my teeth and down my chin, which I think is incredibly sensual.

Besides that, you have to consider the character of Gloria—I don't think she would have swallowed just any guy's sperm. She would have wanted her lover's or her husband's; she'd have wanted the cream of the guy she loved. If she hadn't been abducted from the hotel that night and had gone out with her boyfriend, as planned, she very well may have swallowed all the semen she could get from his cock, but that's not the way the story went. The scene wasn't a love scene!

Come to think of it, the scene was probably the highest form of male chauvinist fantasy ever filmed. Which is a great turn-on for men and women both. Every woman dreams of being violated and forced into submission; every guy dreams of forcing a chick into submission and violating her as he pleases. Every guy dreams of picking up a wholesome-looking girl and forcing her, by his sheer macho power, to submit to his coming all over her face. Every woman dreams of being that wholesome-looking chick, of having no say in what's happening. If there had been sound in the picture at that point—dialogue as opposed to music, I mean (remember, I never uttered one word in the film)—and one of the guys ordered me to swallow his load, I would have. But the way it was done, it was meant to run down my cheeks and drip onto my shoulders and mat in my hair. I think it's so much more exciting to see in the finished film than it would have been had I gobbled it all up, burped, and said,

"Ummm, what a nice snack!" The whole thing—that scene, the entire flick—is an incredible dream. A guy told me, "To have a gorgeous chick prostrate in front of you, knowing she has to submit to any kinky fantasy you like, is probably the *best* fantasy a guy can imagine. It usually never happens in life and that's what makes it so damn exciting on the screen." I'll take it a step further—I'd say it very seldom happens in the marriage bed. How many guys' wives let them beat off on their faces? How many? Probably very few.

And that's where the real importance of *Green Door* and others like it lies—in the fact that because of viewing the film a person will better his sex life. It loosens people up, breaks down their inhibitions and fears, and even teaches them totally new things. A woman once told me: "Honey, I've been married seventeen years next Friday, and I never even knew it was possible to do all that! I'm going to make the next seventeen years the spiciest yet!" And she was telling the truth; she was excited as could be.

Take the last moments of *Green Door* again—the come shots. Maybe a couple will see the film and go home and try it, the girl will let her lover cream onto her face without sucking his cock. And things can go on from there—he could kiss her immediately after he comes and then he can lick his own sperm from her eyelids and her lips. Guys don't realize it, but tasting your own semen can be very exciting. How do I know? I've been told, and I've seen it happen. A guy creams, starts licking it himself, and his cock immediately hardens again—isn't that saying something? And the chick likes it too. It's a wonderful turn-on to have your boyfriend lapping your face, knowing he's licking up his own semen with his tongue, kissing you at the same time.

When you do a film like *Green Door* your fantasy center opens up to a point where you hadn't been before, you find new and interesting things to do in bed. All the time we filmed, I was faithful to my man, Doug. I know that sounds hard to believe but it's true. You know why I was faithful? Because our sex life was wonderfully satisfying—*because* of the film. We would try things I'd learned while filming and we never got bored with each other. It's kind of like the wife who works in an office and one of her fellow secretaries says, "Honey, I've got a great new recipe for you," and you take it from her and she says, "Try it tonight, he'll go crazy!" So you go to the market and then home and cook it and your husband goes berserk over it....

Well, I learned some new techniques for making love, new ways of fucking, new positions, ways of sucking a cock, little touches I hadn't known about before, and I'd take them home and try them on Doug. He'd stretch out (gladly, because he was always as horny as I was) and I'd try my new "recipe" on him. He usually loved it, and the whole week would be filled with variations on that theme, and then we'd go on to something new. So I know sex films can do so much for couples with problems in bed or for couples who are just a little bored with the straight fucking they've been doing for God knows how long. I know because making those sex films did wonders for my sex life with my husband, and we'd had a good one to start with!

I suppose people imagine that making porno films is one of the juiciest things anyone could be involved in, but that isn't true. The people who worked on and in *Green Door* were very liberal and together, sexually, so there were no frustrations to get in the way of work. They were all extremely professional in their outlook, beginning with the Mitchell brothers. Never once did they try to make me, nor did they once think of me as Sally Slut. I was a hired actress and was treated as one. They respected me and they in turn were respected by me. They were very honest guys, never trying to put me on, and that's what turned me on to them. No matter how successful *Green Door* had been, I would never have done *The Resurrection of Eve* if I hadn't gained respect for Jim and Artie Mitchell.

Porno film sets are not the free-for-all, sexual wonderlands people imagine them to be. The atmosphere must be relaxed and informal so that sex scenes will "happen" and have the look and feel of reality, but everyone realizes they are doing a job for which they are paid. Usually everyone goes their separate ways after a day's shooting, unless they're married or living together or something, because they don't have the sexual hang-ups of most middle-class people (and most people working on fuck films are pretty much middle-class, or come from that kind of background). They don't get all hot and bothered by what was filmed that day and run out together and have a wild orgy that tops anything yet seen on camera. They take their horniness or sexiness or whatever you want to call it home with them. Just as I did with Doug. Johnnie Keyes didn't mean anything to me, sexually, off-screen. He was just another actor, a costar, a coworker, a nice guy. If we'd done something in that day's shooting which excited me—say, he'd taught me a new kind of thrust with his cock and it felt different than anything I'd ever felt in my pussy before—I'd go home to Doug that evening and say, "Hey, I had the best feeling today..." and we'd recreate the scene and we'd do it and it would be super wonderful because now I was doing it with the guy I loved and that made it the best.

Was *Behind the Green Door* the best? I don't know; I'm too close to it to tell. And I don't think we'll know what the ultimate porno film is till years from now, when we can look back objectively. I do know that a stroke of luck—the Ivory Snow boxes with my face appearing smack on the front arriving in the supermarkets at the very time when *Green Door* opened in major cities—helped make it the phenomenon it is today. As I'm writing this in New York City, it's playing at three theaters and has been for as long as I can remember. And they tell me there's no end in sight. Fifteen outlying theaters also have it, suburban theaters surrounding New York. I'm astounded every time I think of its success—and I admit I love it. Thank God for Ivory Snow! I do think the film would have caught on anyway, perhaps not as well as it did, but it was too good to be ignored. It was moderately successful even without the free publicity from Procter & Gamble, so I think it would have stood on its own. A review I like to quote sums up that feeling, and also touches on what I mentioned earlier, that the film isn't the essence of perfection: "*Behind the Green Door*, the latest from the Mitchell brothers, seems headed for whammo biz in opening here [San Francisco]. Porno is gradually getting respectable. The Mitchell brothers are imaginative filmmakers who have lavished $50,000 on this feature, their biggest budget so far. The money shows in technical quality. The camera moves are smooth and the Mitchells never fall back on the long, tedious grind stretches that fill many other films. In *Green Door*, moreover, they use slow motion and visual effects to elaborate a few seconds of sexual reaction that normally shoot by in typical pornos. Still, even $50,000 isn't enough to make a good picture, and the brothers are stuck with the results. But with a first-week gross approaching $20,000 in a theater they also own, their cinematic shortcomings are probably acceptable to them."

Another reviewer said:

"Besides being 99 & 44/100% pure profit, *Behind the Green Door* has several things that most sex films ignore. These can be summarized as correct exposure, plot, characterization, a bit of dramatic action to leaven large amounts of hard-core action, and a sense of humor that endeavors to counter the inexpressible tedium that afflicts most sexually explicit films."

What do I say? *Green Door* is a film about fantasy. It's an honest movie about things that are not real, except that a lot of people wish they were real. The film tries to be objective about sex and fantasies, tries to say that sex is nothing to be embarrassed about. I mean, sex is definitely here to stay—in the cinema and elsewhere. Hollywood is putting more sex into their movies not because they *want* to, but because they *have to*. It's not something the filmmakers are trying to cram down peoples' throats. It's what people want to see.

I'm very honest when it comes to sex. I can use words like *cocksucker* and *fuck* because they are very natural to me. But things were not always that way. Marilyn Chambers was once Marilyn Briggs, as uptight a small-town girl as you could imagine. And now perhaps it's time to tell you about where this walking package of opposing forces—the essence of purity and princess of porn—came from, and what she was all about before you ever heard of her....

2

High School and Losing My Virginity

"**H**er beauty is very American in an ephemeral way," someone once wrote of me. "It is difficult to remember what she looks like when not looking at her. Pleasing, but not yet old enough to have developed its own distinct character. It is the perfect face for advertising and the screen—at once striking and anonymous. Like the girl next door who is the head cheerleader at the high school, marries the star quarterback (as handsome as a Greek god), supports him through a business major at the state college, and, while he goes on to success in real estate, bears him two perfect children and fades slowly into the suburbs, her beauty is the emblem of the American nightmare from which millions cannot awake."

Difficult to live up to.

But very effective for selling soap.

Much of the above statement is true. I am the girl next door, I was the head cheerleader, my first sexual experience was with the star quarterback, and I did support a husband and live in the suburbs. But let's go back a bit:

15

I'm a Taurus, born April 22, 1952, in Providence, Rhode Island, but my parents moved to Westport, Connecticut, when I was about six months old, so I always say I'm from Westport and leave it at that. We lived in one house for about fifteen years and then we moved into the house my parents have today. And that's it. Very typical American, right?

I had a good childhood, a good family life. My brother, Bill, is twenty-eight now, and my sister, Janice, is twenty-seven. Which means I'm the baby of the family. I guess I'd have to say that they were closer to each other than to me because of the closeness of their ages. I mean, they had five years together before I was even around.

When I say I have a brother and sister I immediately get asked, "How have they reacted?" I'm not sure whether people are asking that about my success in general or about the fact that their little sisters aren't supposed to do that, even in the bedroom.

The reaction has been very positive. My brother has been in show business and he knows what it's about, so he kind of admires what's happened, admires my ambition. I guess there's a little envy, which is only natural (I think it exists between all brothers and sisters, whether it has anything to do with show business or not), but it isn't jealousy.

My brother used to play with a band called Barry and the Remains. They had a kind of moderate success—they cut an album and a single, were on the *Ed Sullivan Show*, things like that. He's always been into music and he always will be, even though he now sells Porsches. He's always been very into cars too. It makes life interesting, doing different things. We're alike in many ways, always "on," ready to live like crazy. He's married now and has a child and he's happy—and happy for me.

My sister is a housewife and we're not particularly close, but that has nothing to do with my career and the things I've done. She's of another generation—my brother is too—and that's the generation that reads *Playboy* but isn't ready to see their baby sister having intercourse or giving head on the silver screen. So I don't think they will ever quite understand.

I've always been a show-off and I think they resent that a bit, and that's just a carry-over from childhood days. My sister would probably say she's the black sheep of the family (I guess because she's the middle child and the middle child's always supposed to be the "different" one), but the truth is I'm the one who sticks out. I was a show-off and I got attention and I loved it, and I suppose that has a lot to do with my act today and my love of applause from the audience. It has to be in you, a part of you, or you can't make it. It was always a part of me, and my brother and sister resented it a little.

I was very proud of my brother when his band was doing well. He was cutting records, travelling, and making a lot of money and I was thrilled that he was my brother and I could walk around and tell people that, but I felt a little tinge of envy too, so I think I know exactly how he feels today. I'd feel the same way if we reversed roles.

I remember one time my sister and I had a terrific argument; I mean we hated each other and swore we wouldn't share the same room any longer. We told our mom and demanded that we be split up, that somehow, magically, we get separate rooms, but there were no extra rooms in the house. So we came up with this outrageous scheme that would allow us to live in the same room but never have to go near each other. (We weren't speaking, so we didn't even want to look at each other.)

We strung a rope across the room, between our beds, the line of demarcation, and her side was her side and mine was mine. We hung blankets on the rope for a few days so we didn't have to look at each other, but finally they fell down. It was crazy. She'd drop something on my side and I'd go nuts and scream and throw it back at her, or she'd find that something of hers had fallen over to my side and I refused to give it back (squatter's rights!) and wouldn't let her reach over to my turf to grab it.

One day neither one of us could remember what we had originally fought about, what the big deal was that had caused the division of the room in the first place. So we took it down and made up. We had good times when we were kids, good times fighting and good times making up. A more normal childhood you couldn't ask for—birthday parties, wonderful holiday celebrations, vacations together. I wouldn't have traded it for anything in the world.

Then there are my parents, the people basically responsible for making my childhood a good one and respecting my desire to make something of my life and allowing me to begin modeling in New York while still in high school. I'm asked the same thing over and over again: "How have your parents reacted?"

"To what?" I say.

"You know ... the ...uh, movies." The person usually blushes, waiting for some violent answer about my parents refusing to even acknowledge *Green Door*'s existence.

Well, the fact is, my parents are proud of me in their own way. By that, I mean I haven't become famous in quite the way a mother and father would like their daughter to become famous, but they respect my ambition and success and applaud it nonetheless. See, what people are really asking when they say, "How have your parents reacted?" is, "What do your mom and dad say about you sucking cock on screen?"

The answer, I'm sorry to say to all those who want to be told a titillating story, is that they don't say anything. I'm sure my mom has not seen my films and I don't think she should. She isn't ready for them. I don't know about my dad. He's an advertising man in New York and I would imagine the temptation to drop in at a double bill of *Green Door* and *Eve* at lunchtime would be hard to fight. I think he's seen them because of a story that filtered back to me:

One afternoon soon after the film (*Green Door*) had come out some friends of my dad took him to see it. He didn't know who the star was. And he freaked out. I don't know if he walked out but I heard that he really wasn't ready for it. I don't know if that story's true, I mean it's only a rumor, but I could see it happening.

I really do think he's seen the films since then, probably alone. He (and my mother too) has become so much more liberal in the past few years, so much more cool. People are cooling out, becoming less uptight with things in life, especially things like sex and pornography, which aren't really the big deals they've been cracked up to be.

My parents understand that I've always had a strong will and that no one has ever told me how to live my life. They respect that in me just as I respect their lives and don't want to infringe upon that by writing about them for hours. They're concerned with me and what I do; they worry a little because I'm their baby—it's as simple as that. My mom is probably even more concerned and sometimes worries about me because she's a nurse, a very fine one, and I think she chose that field because she has great empathy for people and their problems; she cares very deeply about people. Especially her children.

We have a good relationship. I see them as often as I can and we talk and relax and when I speak of the future, I can see their eyes light up. They like Chuck a lot, probably because he's the kind of person they respect—outgoing, strong, and genuinely warm. My dad feels especially comfortable with him and they get along as though they've been buddies for years. Chuck is the antithesis of Doug, my ex-husband. Doug was a follower and Chuck is a leader. My parents dig that. They trust Chuck to take good care of me. With Doug, it was the other way around—I took care of him—and my mom and dad could never quite understand that.

My mom once told me, "Marilyn, you'll never stop doing the unexpected, will you? No, you won't." She answered it herself, and I was glad because it told me that she understood and perhaps even liked the idea that my life would be full of surprises for her (and for me too). When I bought my home in Beverly Hills Chuck and I invited my parents out for a week and they came. Buying a $100,000 house was unexpected for a daughter who not too many years before had been waiting tables in dives in San Francisco, and my parents dug it. They even accepted the fact that Chuck and I weren't married but lived together as though we were, a fact that would have upset them a lot just a few years before.

I think my parents and my brother and sister are trembling because I'm writing a book ("What's she going to say about us?"), but relax, I love you all and you know it. And I want everyone to know it. I have a good family, a wonderful family, and I wouldn't be where I am today without that family.

They always let me do what I wanted, my parents never tried to stop me (though they offered good advice, which I sometimes didn't take and later realized I should have), and my brother and sister never tried to discourage me. I went to church for about eight years (we were Congregationalists) and then quit. They asked why and I told them I just didn't feel it was doing anything for me, and that was that. Since then my parents have stopped going too.

So I wasn't brought up in a strict religious home, thank God, if you don't mind me phrasing it that way. You know what, though? I was going to turn Catholic at one point. I had a girlfriend who was Catholic and we used to play "nuns" and things like that.

More than that, I had fantasies of *becoming a nun*! I did, I really wanted to become a nun. Can you see that? *Sister Marilyn*. Wow! I'm not sure what made the Catholic Church so attractive to me; I know I didn't really consciously think about it. I didn't say, "Yeah, those robes and all that glitz turn me on." I think it was more the mysteriousness of it, and the majesty. And the authority that went with it. I felt a nun had a kind of morbid authority, a ruling ability, and she was someone people almost bowed to and revered.

It was theater again. That theatrical childhood that leads to a career in show business. Playing "nuns" was acting out a fantasy, just as being raped and ravished in the nude in *Green Door* was acting out a fantasy from high school. I was always doing "plays" in garages, getting in front of an audience, making up things as we went along. It was great fun and very constructive too.

And sports. Wow, I love sports. And I don't mean only bedroom sports! I always craved competition (Linda Lovelace, more over) and liked being involved in a game rather than having to watch it. If I could have gone out for football, I would have. But I couldn't, so I did the next closest thing—I became a cheerleader. I loved to swim and did a lot of diving, competed in gymnastics. Filming the trapeze number in *Green Door* was a gas for me because all the time I was beating those guys off on either side of me, I wanted to jump on one of them (the trapeze bars, not the guys!) and swing through the air ... with the greatest ease. And I never lost in any competition, except I came in second once, but I don't count that. See, I am telling the truth in this book.

Who were my heartthrobs as I was growing up, as I was shedding my young and innocent role for that of a worldlier, big-city girl? Ricky Nelson. Oh, I'd watch Ozzie and Harriet, his suit forever pressed, her hair never having known wind, and Ricky would walk into the room in his collegiate sweater and I'd gasp and feel a tingle (I won't tell you where!) and I'd nearly pass out when he sang. And Dr. Kildare, Richard Chamberlain. Wow, he knocked me out! Elvis, Fabian. My sister was even nutsier about movie stars than I was. She had all the fan magazines, which meant I didn't have to buy my own (except for when we lived in a divided room). I always loved animals and nature and trees. In fact, while I'm writing this Chuck and I are thinking of giving up the house in Los Angeles for a home near Lake Tahoe, where the air is still clear and the trees green and the skies blue.

I'm a home person. I've been on the road for so long I almost don't know what that's like any longer, but I'm sure I'll get back into it. She'll hate me for saying it, but my mom isn't the world's greatest cook. Maybe that's the reason I love cooking so much, and I'm pretty good at it. There's a lot of housewife in me, I guess. But I couldn't do it over a long period of time. My concentration level is very intense when I do something I find interesting, but if I do it over and over again for days, I easily get distracted. So I like to cook in spurts rather than day after day.

Just as there's a lot of housewife in me, there's a lot of adventure too. For instance, I don't find making cheese sandwiches very exciting, but I get off on whipping up a big fancy Italian meal. Italian food's my favorite.

Hmmm. I lost my virginity after an Italian dinner. Wonder if that has anything to do with it?

My virginity. Yes, I was born a virgin and remained one till the ripe age of seventeen. I masturbated like crazy, but I couldn't get up the guts to "go all the way" with a boy, even though I came close many times. That puritan ethic hung strong in the New England air.

I remember it and I laugh. The whole thing was so dumb, so ridiculous. You know how you prepare yourself, in your mind, for your first fuck ... Rick Nelson meets you on the beach and so you're smiling at him as he takes you in his arms and before you know it you're both naked and he swears eternal love to you and the violins play and the bells ring and you're carried out to sea on a raft of pleasure. *As the World Turns. Search For Tomorrow. The Young And the Restless.*

Well, my Rick Nelson wasn't a Rick Nelson, believe me, and our raft sank in midstream.

Let me start out by saying I was a cockteaser in high school. I think every chick who runs for homecoming queen in every high school in America is a pricktease. That's how she gets nominated, and the one who carries it off the best, the one who keep the guys hard (but four feet away from her body) the longest is the one who wins the crown.

So the cockteaser (me) finally gave in to the good-looking jock (Tony). After an Italian meal.

I'd known him for years and he was always kind or an idol to me, athletic, strong, good-looking, but not nearly as beautiful a Ricky or Richard or Elvis or Fabian. He'd always treated me as kind of a baby sister (he was basically a friend of my brother) and then suddenly I realized he wanted to get into my pants. And I wanted to get into his. So we started dating and moving toward sex at a very slow pace. He was really impressed that I was going to New York all the time and doing some modeling, which made me seem very worldly and all, but inside I was an uptight virgin who had fantasies of black guys raping her while she masturbated. Normal, right? I don't know what his fantasies were, but they sure couldn't beat (in humor anyway) our first night of sex.

It was a real big deal. I mean we both knew this was going to be the night of reckoning. "Either you put out for me or forget it, Marilyn Briggs." That was his attitude and I didn't blame him. I'd been leading him into making that take-it-or-leave-it statement. I'd let him French kiss me (My God, but that phrase sounds so antiquated these days!) and then I'd moan and purr and pull his hand away every time he reached for my right breast (he was left-handed and I think he didn't even know how to use his right hand; he was always playing with my right breast, never seemed to know the other one existed) and when he'd start going down between my legs (with his left hand again, not his mouth), I'd move away and tell him, "I can't Tony, I just can't!"

And I didn't help any, because I'd slide my fingers down to his belt and play with it, lightly touching his stomach and his thighs, pretending to be madly in love with his crummy belt when actually it was the little feels of his hard cock I was after, and it drove him nuts. I think he came in his undershorts twice when we were doing all that foreplay stuff, but I never had enough nerve to ask him. Why did I think that? 'Cause on two different occasions he suddenly shuddered, right in the middle of our passionate kissing and feeling, straightened up with a, "Wow, Marilyn, it's really getting late..." and started the car and whisked me home. Figure it out.

Anyhow, that couldn't go on forever, and I was dying to do it, to go all the way. I wondered if he'd ever done it with a girl before, and years later, when we met one day in Westport, we talked about our one and only time in the sack, we *laughed* about it, and he admitted that I was his first. I think all the high school jocks were virgins and their locker room talk was just a lot of fantasy bullshit. But I guess that's healthy.

I wonder if Tony ever talked about me in the locker room. I doubt it. He wouldn't have been able to keep a straight face. Our "lovemaking" was like something out of a Woody Allen movie.

We drove to a park on the edge of Westport, both smelling like garlic and oregano, and killed the lights. It was raining, so Tony left the car running and the heater on low and the fan on high so that we'd stay warm and wouldn't suffocate. We started to hold each other and kiss and touch, an instant replay of what we'd been doing for months, and it was as difficult as ever in his car because he had bucket seats and a console.

I let him put his hand on my right breast this time with no pushing away. He went nuts. We nearly bit off each other's tongues. Finally he had my blouse open and my bra unhitched (those are long-gone days, when I wore a bra, and Tony, of course, unlatched it with his left hand) and he was feeling me and kissing my chin and then my neck and finally he put his lips on my nipple and I went crazy. I reached down between his legs and placed my hand right smack on the lump in his pants. He moaned and became as nuts as I was. Then he moved his wild left hand down under my skirt and pulled away.

"Come on, Marilyn…"

"Tony, I just can't!"

"I *love* you!"

"I love you too, Tony, but I –"

He slammed his mouth on mine and I wrapped my fingers around the hard thing in his pants and he moved his fingers up under my skirt and felt my damp panties (and they weren't damp for the rain.).

"Pleeeeeeeese," he moaned.

"Oh … Tony … no, not all the way!"

Then it happened. Just as lightning lit up the trees around us he said, "Either you put out for me or forget it, Marilyn Briggs," in his deepest, most masculine tone.

I thought about it. Not for long. An ultimatum, right?

"Yes, Tony," I think I gasped, "I want to, I really do!" I probably added something like, "Please be gentle," or some such crap.

So we spent about half an hour yanking at each other's clothes. We thought we had to kiss all through it, so it was the longest kiss on record. We kept our lips glued as we fought buttons and hooks and buckles and bucket seats and that damned shift knob sticking up between us. I think he ended up with his pants and undershorts down around his ankles and I had one shoe left on and my skirt crumpled around it.

So the rain was beating down and we were trying to get into some kind of position to make love. I wrapped my hand around his cock (first time, remember, and I was amazed at the size of it and how hard and warm it felt) and he slid a finger up me and we kept kissing like crazy all through it, sweating, huffing, and puffing....

I guess there was some kind of unwritten rule that you didn't speak when trying to make love for the first time (some people never speak when making love, come to think of it), so we did everything with hand gestures and little pushes and shoves in this direction or that. You'd think we were deaf, dumb, and blind, I swear. He tried to lift me over the console but it didn't quite work out. So we broke the silence and I think I said, "How are we going to do it?"

"The back seat?" he asked.

We both looked back there. It was smaller than the front, with bucket seats no less, and anyway it was piled with books and football helmets and stuff like that. So we tried to stretch out in the front seat again. Tony got up on his knees on the seat, which was no easy trick because of the steering wheel, and started to lower himself to me as I lifted my legs over the console and attempted to lie on those contours as if the whole thing were a flat bed. My neck was breaking (it was pressing against the arm rest on the door), my back felt as though it would snap at any moment because the seat was concave, my ass was on the console (which was the only good part of it, because my pussy was up high and it would be easy for him to enter me), my legs were under the steering wheel....

Tony whispered something about it not hurting and how I shouldn't be afraid and I guess we really thought that that position was going to work because I had my arms up around his neck and he was coming down at me and I could feel the tip of his penis already touching between my legs and we were trembling in excitement and then....

I got my goddamned foot caught in the horn. All of a sudden, blaaaat! Like a trumpet in the night! I didn't even realize it was us, I mean I didn't know our car was making that noise, I didn't know it was my foot. I got scared and Tony jumped as if someone had just goosed him. "Marilyn, move your foot!"

"What?"

He was struggling to stay on his knees and pull my foot out of the steering wheel. "Shit, Marilyn, get your foot off the goddamned horn!"

"I can't!" It was stuck. And worse than that, it was hurting.

Well, the horn wouldn't stop and dumb Tony finally pulled up on the horn thing, the rim or whatever it is, and I thought he'd sliced off my toe and I screamed and kicked and that finally got my foot free and the stupid thing stopped blaring. God, it was suddenly so quiet.

"Shit," he mumbled, looking around, waiting for a thousand policemen to drive up and open the doors and ask us what the hell was wrong.

"Tony, it's okay, look, I'll get back into position."

"Oh ... Marilyn, I love you...."

So he got into position again, rubbing my pussy lips with his cock, and I pressed my abdomen into the air above the console as he came down to me ... slowly ... slowly ... and then...

Tony slipped. He had been balancing his entire weight on his hands, one on the part of the console that extended into the back seat, the other on the little bit of console left next to my rear, next to the shift knob. That's the hand that slipped. He suddenly let out a yell any football player would be ashamed of and crashed down on top of me. For a second I thought maybe he'd suddenly gone into a Tarzan number and wanted to shove it into me like a gorilla—but I knew he'd missed 'cause nothing was touching my pussy but his abdomen.

That was trouble enough. But a disaster always needs a final touch to make it memorable. Tony's hand had slipped off the console and hit the shift knob. The car had been running and he hadn't set the parking brake—he hadn't even set the gearshift in the park position, he'd put it in neutral. Well, it went from neutral to drive in one fast move and we soon realized we were going for a ride. There we were, tangled up in our clothes, in that backbreaking position, and the car was moving and the rain was pelting down.

Tony tried to get up, saying, "Jesus, oh, Christ!" and I couldn't help but laugh. I mean I was hysterical, so scared I was finding everything comical. He tried desperately to find the brake pedal as the car chugged through the mud—"Marilyn, move your fucking legs!" (my feet were still down under the steering wheel)—and just as I lifted my feet to the dashboard and squealed with laughter he slammed his foot down and instead of the brake pedal he got the accelerator. Maybe he should have used his left hand.

Well, the engine made this tremendous noise and we really didn't go anywhere. The wheels just dug down into the muck and then a nice big tree stopped any further progress; the car went dead. I slid to the floor, my naked buttocks hitting his cold, wet floor mats, my feet up behind the steering wheel, the shift knob between my legs, and my head against the window crank.

Tony slumped back in the seat and said, "Shit."

Well, I cracked up again. There we were, the young lovers, suave and sophisticated, the guy sitting behind the steering wheel of his nearly wrecked and half-sunk-in-the-mud-car, his pants in a ball on the floor, his cock still sticking up in excitement, the girl on the floor in some yoga position, her ass wet (he had a leak in the windshield on the passenger side), and her dreams of Ricky Nelson suddenly vanishing into the giggles.

Tony helped me up and asked if I was okay, which was nice of him, and I said I was, still laughing, which I don't think he appreciated all that much, and then he turned on the lights 'cause it was pitch dark except for the lightning and we had to see what the hell we were doing. We tried to get back into our clothes as discreetly as possible, which was silly, but we were both very embarrassed. We kept bumping each other as we dressed, saying "excuse me" and "I'm sorry" all the time the car was sinking into the mud.

Tony tried to start the car but it wouldn't do anything but make a terrible noise so he got out and told me he was going to get help. And that was it. *Bang*. He slammed the door and left me sitting there in that cold car in the rain, with the mud nearly over the wheels, and my hysterical laughter turned to hysterical crying and I finally got so upset and scared I actually screamed out loud, "I want my mother!" I even tried to get out of the car and catch up with Tony, but my feet sank ankles-deep in the mud and that made me cry even more.

About half an hour later, I saw a light flashing through the trees. I immediately thought, Oh, no, the cops! And I had visions of being dragged into the police station and my parents having to come there in their nightclothes and everyone calling me a whore and a tramp. But the light was yellow, meaning it was a tow truck (Tony had found another car—I think the couple in the car were fucking and he knocked on the window—and asked for a ride to a service station).

So I sat in the front of this big tow truck, rubbing the mud off my ankles as Tony and the driver pulled the car out of the mush and back onto the blacktop of the parking lot.

Some night for losing one's virginity, huh?

But I did.

Yes, I know it sounds crazy, and it was. I was so mad, so furious, as we drove home that I wouldn't even talk to Tony. He kept apologizing and saying, "Marilyn, it wasn't my fault, I love you, I really do." And I just looked the other way and watched the street signs to make sure he was taking me directly to my house. But as soon as we turned onto my street, I realized what a wreck I was and how was I going to explain how I looked to my parents?

I panicked. "Tony, I have to take a shower at your house!"

"Wha … what?"

"I can't go home, my mom and dad would kill me, and my brother'd kill you!"

"Oh. Yeah, well, sure."

And we drove to his house. The reason I had no qualms about taking a shower at his house was because he'd told me at dinner that his parents were out of town for the weekend, in New York at some convention or something.

So I showered—with the door locked. I washed my shoes and everything. It was ridiculous. Finally, I emerged from the bathroom to find that he had taken a shower in his parent's bathroom and suddenly he looked fresh and attractive and my juices started flowing again. So did his. But I didn't want to admit it.

We walked around the house whispering—I didn't know why, but I sure found out later—as though the ghosts of his parents were walking around and the place gave me the creeps and it was getting late so I told him I wanted to go home.

We got into the car and he started it and turned on the heater and windshield wipers, but we didn't go anywhere. He kept telling me how sorry he was and how much he really loved me and pretty soon we were both laughing over the crazy incident and before we knew it, we were kissing again. I guess we were both so hot to fuck that nothing would have stopped us. It was as simple as that. And we were willing to go to any lengths to do it. Even to the point of attempting to do it in the front seat of the car again! How's that for insanity?

This time it wasn't quite so bad. Trial and error is a good teacher. We knew a little better where to move our feet and where to put our heads and how to balance and how to keep excited all through those maneuvers. This time we took it slowly and easily and Tony made sure the shift knob was in the park position. We got out of our clothes completely this time and tossed them in the back seat with the football helmets and books. It started getting very romantic, the rain and all, the rhythm of the windshield wipers, the radio on nice and soft. The thunder crackled and when the lightning lit up the sky I could see Tony's strong body above me, his hard chest and the thick hair above his cock and all and it really turned me on. I gave in, completely. "Take me, I'm yours!" That kind of thing.

Then he bent forward and kissed my right nipple (even his face was left-handed) and then I felt his prick pressing into my cunt. It was the first time and it felt better than I'd dreamed it would. My fingers or anything I'd used to masturbate with never felt so terrific. I started moaning and he did too and he slid into me and I squealed in pain and clawed at his back and….

"Christ! Don't move, keep quiet!" Tony suddenly said, his eyes wide, his face suddenly lit up, and not by lightning. A car was coming up the driveway behind us and he slammed his body down on mine, nearly snapping my spine on the console, and I lay there with his hand over my mouth, frightened out of my mind, suddenly and completely pulled out of my first real sexual experience by a damned searchlight! It was bad enough that our initial attempt had been aborted by a slippery hand and lots of mud, but to have it happen again in the same evening? We really were crazy!

As the car came closer and closer I felt that big thing inside of me getting smaller and smaller, and finally, when I heard a car door slam, I felt Tony's cock slip out. He tensed and waited for someone to open the car door and slap him on the ass, I guess, but all we heard was the back door of the house close tightly, and then Tony said, "Wow, that was close."

I mumbled something and then he realized I was suffocating with his hand on my mouth, so he got up and so did I, and I was pissed, really pissed. "Who the hell was that? I asked, grabbing my panties from the back seat.

"My brother. I thought he was home already."

"Oh, that's why you were whispering in there."

"Yeah ... hey, Marilyn, you're not –"

"*I hat your guts!*"

"Shhh!"

"Go to hell!" Man, was I mad!

But not mad enough. Man enough in the crazy sense, which would soon be proven, but mad in the furious sense that he had put me through two very trying situations. Losing one's virginity is a serious matter and this was turning out to be the comedy act of the century.

I got dressed as he sat there, naked, playing with himself (with his left hand), telling me how much he loved me (again), and asking me to go into the house with him, to his room, where it would be safe and we would have a nice bed and we could do what we'd started to do.

Well, I was dying for it more than I was mad at him, and seeing him sitting there playing with his penis was enough to make me want to go down on him (which I'd never done in my life and knew "good girls" were never supposed to do). So I gave in and he scooped up his clothes and bundled them up in his arms, turned off the engine, slid into his loafers, and we made a mad dash through the rain to the back door, only to find that it was locked for the night. His brother had seen his car, figured he was in for the night, and locked the door.

Great.

I said, "I think you'd better take me home."

"Marilyn," he moaned, and kissed me and I could feel his cock getting hard again and I was trembling with excitement and knew I really didn't want him to take me home. So we ran around to the front of the house—he was still naked—and tried that door. It too was locked. So there we were, in the storm of all storms, a naked football player and his clothed but very wet girlfriend, wondering how the hell to get into the house. For some idiotic reason that I can't remember, he didn't have a key to the house on the chain with the car keys. His precious car had its own precious chain for its own precious keys.

Finally, he climbed in through a window, into the kitchen, and came around to the back door and opened it for me. I was drenched. I looked the same as I'd looked after the scene in the woods, except for the mud to my ankles. So I started to cry and I said, "It's not supposed to be like this."

"It'll be beautiful," he said, and got a big towel to wrap around my head while he took my blouse and skirt and underwear off (for the third time that night—no, fourth time, if you count my undressing to take a shower). He rubbed me with the towel all over and I felt warm and happy again and excited. We kissed there in the kitchen and shared a beer to warm us up and then we started feeling each other all over and finally he said, "Let's go to bed."

I just nodded. It was finally going to happen, and happen right! I followed him up the steps in ecstasy.

When we reached the second floor he whispered, "Be real quiet, don't make a sound. I don't want to wake my brother." I didn't know his brother, but I knew that my sister did, and all I needed was for his brother to catch us fucking and tell my sister!

"Where's your room?" I whispered.

"Follow me. I don't want to put any lights on 'cause Bob might wake up."

It made sense. The house was dark and we were both sure that his brother had gone right to bed. So I held his hand and he opened the door to his room and we went in and he closed it. All without a word. The shade had been pulled down, and it was the kind that blocks out all the light—so even the lightning didn't penetrate it. I was glad for that because the lightning only reminded me of the scenes in the car, and also because I had always figured sex should take place in a romantic, dark-dark-dark bedroom. I couldn't see a thing but I knew I almost tipped over a set of barbells and clothes lying on the floor, but that excited me 'cause it was so masculine, just like my brother's room. The place even smelled masculine. Probably had some sweat sox lying around or something.

Anyhow, he led me to the bed, all the time saying, "Shhh," which I didn't understand 'cause I hadn't made a sound, and I didn't think the walls were that thin. Maybe he was talking to the springs in the mattress. I didn't know.

I put my head on the pillow and realized that I was lying a pile of paperback books, so I had to push them aside, and they fell to the floor and he froze and said, "Shhhhhhhhh!"

Jesus! What was I supposed to do, stop breathing?

Finally, and it seemed like hours because he was moving so slowly, he positioned himself between my legs and came down to kiss me and enter me at the same time. It hurt for a minute or so and then it started feeling wonderful. I pulled him down on top of me and we really started going at it. I suddenly wiped out all the memories of what had happened earlier in the night and was living only for the moment. I always knew I liked sex, meaning I loved to masturbate, but this was something else and I wondered why I had waited so long to do it. It was great and I could tell he was holding back so he wouldn't come fast and we could keep doing it for a long time. He was as scared as I was but as soon as we realized that it was going to be easy, he knew what he was doing. We kissed and we sweated and pressed our bodies together as we moved in a steady rhythm on the bed.

I realized I was going to have an orgasm and I moaned.

"Shh!"

"Tony, Tony," I whined, feeling his cock pounding into me. I didn't give a damn about being quiet any longer. "Oh, Tony!"

Clamp. The old hand-over-the-mouth routine again. He just clamped my mouth shut. Then, with his cock still in me, he whispered, "If my brother wakes up we're dead."

I nodded. That got him to take his hand off my face. Then I whispered, "How can your brother possibly hear us?"

"What do you mean?"

"You're acting as though he's in this room!"

Ha ha ha. Marilyn really said it that time. You should have seen the look on my face when Tony answered, "He is!"

Yes, across the room, in another twin bed, lay his brother Bob, sound asleep. We were fucking in Tony's room, but Tony never bothered to tell me he shared his room with his brother. The master bedroom was empty, but if he didn't want to do it in his parent's bed, which I could understand, why not the guest bedroom or the living room floor or even a bathtub? The goddamned car would have been safer! We'd walk around with broken backs for the rest of our lives, but we wouldn't have had his brother in the back seat to worry about.

I couldn't believe it. I just kept thinking, you stupid idiot, you stupid jock idiot asshole! And he kept fucking me! Like crazy, just as long as I didn't make a sound. I liked the way it felt, even though it was still hurting, but my head was no longer into it. The craziest night of my life had culminated with a situation more absurd than anyone could have possibly imagined. An empty house full of empty beds and sofas and soft carpeting, and I have to lose my virginity in a twin bed next to my lover's sleeping brother.

I'll tell you, though, that last moment, just as Tony started to come in me for the first time, was incredible, even if I felt as though I was going to choke because I wasn't breathing. He slammed his cock into me, his body shook, and I could feel it jerking as the cream poured out and I dug my nails into his strong back and bit down hard on his shoulder. It was a great moment, and we turned on our side in our passion, which wasn't the best move to make....

We fell right to the goddamned floor, right on top of the paperback books. My foot hit the barbells and his cock slipped out of me and I could feel it still spraying all over my stomach and we still hugged each other in passionate silence. But it was over. The fall had finished the magic. And when I finally let my arms fall to the floor, when I finally relaxed, to top it all off, I got my fingers tangled in a jock strap.

Don't ever lose your virginity to a football player. It isn't worth the hassle.

Well, I was glad it was over. I now knew what fucking was like, and how ridiculous an evening you had been building yourself up for could be. Our silent drive home to my house in the rain was very heavy—Tony didn't know what to say to make me happy and I didn't know exactly how I felt. Everything had gone wrong, but some of it had felt nice. I pretended to be madder than I really was and I slammed the car door without a word and crept into the house just as the sun was beginning to rise. I crawled into bed and thought I would cry myself to sleep.

Not so. I giggled instead. It really was too funny for tears.

I ached for a week. That was the rough part. I think I walked around bowlegged and sore. But it had been worth it, even though it had been such a disaster. I had finally "gone all the way" and I had liked it.

And a few weeks later, I found myself doing it again. No football player this time, no cars, no brothers, just a nice, good-looking, normal, average student. It was great. A great fuck. And just about all of them have been since.

Sex is terrific, even if your first shot at it makes you laugh.

3

Cheerleading, Homecoming and Making a Movie

In a small town when the head cheerleader gets kicked off the team for drinking beer it creates somewhat of a scandal. It happened to me. But I thought it was a gas.

Cheerleading for me was more a release of physical energy than dedication to school spirit. It was being in front of an audience and having people look at you and know you. I enjoyed it, loved the exercise it gave me, but I never considered it a sacred institution. That's why I was able to say, "Oh, well, big deal," when it all fell in on me.

Cheerleading was a kind of joke, at least to me. It never really meant anything; it was a kind of exhibitionism. I never told anyone that because I never would have made the team if I had. You had to *believe* in cheerleading, you had to *live* for it. I liked the competition you had to go through to get on the team, and once on it I liked the time and energy it took. But I had another life besides cheerleading, and that included cigarettes and beer. And when I say cigarettes, I mean cigarettes, not grass. Grass was around, but it wasn't yet popular.

41

But beer was very popular. You could get it at the state line, and that's where we went. It was fun, it tasted good, we liked it. No big deal. But it was a big deal with the guys on the football and basketball teams. If they got caught drinking beer, or even coming near it, they were kicked off the team. It was as simple as that.

Same thing with the cheerleaders. One day they had this big meeting, the faculty and all, and we were told, "There are rumors that cheerleaders as well as team members have been seen getting beer at the state line. Cheerleading is an honor and cheerleaders must set an example for the rest of the school … blah blah blah." So all of a sudden, just as the coach was telling us, "You are on your *honor*, we don't want rumors or others telling stories, we want each of you to be honest with us," these two chicks stood up, two straight, uptight chicks who had boyfriends on the team, and both of them pointed at me and said, "She's the one!" There I sat, with these two do-gooders pointing at me, ratting on me as the coach is telling us we're on our honor. Amazing.

Well, the coach was in a good mood and he told the two chicks to sit down and shut up, but they were all watching me from that moment on. Like I was going to pull a can of Schlitz out of my pompon and chug it down in front of God and everybody.

Right after that time, after that meeting, I had my tonsils taken out. I needed it too, they were huge. I looked like a chipmunk or squirrel filling his mouth full of nuts to store for the winter. So I went into the hospital and when I got out it was time for basketball season to start. We had cheerleading practice one night after school and I couldn't cheer 'cause my throat was still too sore, but I went through the physical motions. And then it happened. Those same two chicks dragged over the coach and the big bruiser of a women's phys-ed teacher we had and they announced to me that I had been sacked. Why? Those chicks had witnessed me drinking beer the week before. Hah. I'd been in the hospital that week. And I couldn't even argue with them because I couldn't use my voice. So I tossed my pompon in the can and figured, why fight it? I liked beer and was bound to be caught sometime (with those two bloodhounds on my trail, did I have a chance?).

My parents were a little bent out of shape because of it but the charge of having been seen drinking beer was lessened in their eyes by the fact that I had indeed been in a hospital that week in question. My mother was a nurse, so she could attest to that. But it upset them because they never allowed their children to drink, not till we reached twenty-one. Not a drop. So to have the baby daughter getting the reputation of a beer guzzler sat hard on their heads. It was good that it happened, however. It prepared them for the day when they would find out that baby daughter was the star of a porno movie.

Actually, getting kicked off the team was good for me because it gave me a lot more time to work at a career, to work at getting modeling jobs. I've always been in a rush to grow up, all my life, and modeling seemed to me to be going into another world, a very grown-up and mature world. I started finding school functions boring, especially things like running for homecoming queen, which I thought was really corny.

It was. But I did it anyway. How I got nominated I'll never know, because I was never the "Rah, rah, school!" or "Go, team, go!" type. Hmmm. Maybe that's *why* I got nominated—I was different.

Homecoming wasn't such a big deal to anyone, I don't think, not in the way it had been when my sister had been in high school, but we still went through the motions. The dance (which I skipped) and the parade (which was fun) and the crowning at the game (I lost and so did the team). Ex-cheerleader-beer-drinker-model running for homecoming queen! At least it was controversial. Oh, high school. The time of masturbation fantasies and real sex and cheerleading and homecoming. It's all back there somewhere in the past, in a nice memory slot. But the important part of my high school life was breaking into a modeling career.

I started when I was fifteen years old. I know that's young, but even at that age high school in Connecticut bored me. And thank God it was a liberal high school, because I spent most of my afternoons down in New York City. Yes, even though they didn't allow their cheerleaders to drink beer, they allowed them to skip classes. So I looked for modeling jobs while other kids were dissecting fetal pigs. I'd go from one agency to another, asking, "Don't you want a new, fresh young face from Smalltown, USA?" with my biggest smile flashing. I was young and naive. I took acting classes whenever I could and tried (without success) to land a part in an off-Broadway show. I wanted to be in show business in any way, shape, or form. Standing in front of a crowd on bleachers shouting, "Block that pass!" was not my idea of success.

My parents tried to discourage me, of course, but not only because they were parents and they didn't like seeing their little baby girl running down to perverted Manhattan all the time. My dad was in the advertising business so he knew that whole scene of trying to become a model. He knew what he was trying his best to discourage me from entering—the advertising/modeling profession. He knew how rough it was. "Marilyn, it's a lousy business. So what do you want to go down there for [New York]? It's a drag." But I didn't listen. I found it marvelously exciting. While the girls in my class were going to dances at the gym, I was bouncing around New York, portfolio in hand, looking for that one big break....

It was the usual young-model-in-the-big-city routine. I'd see someone at an agency and they'd send me out on an interview and I'd try to get work. I did. I was lucky. I landed quite a few things, more TV commercials than print work, which I thought was odd but very exciting. I modeled fabrics, makeup, all kinds of things. I was one of the members of the Pepsi Generation, I pretended I colored my hair with Clairol, washing and drying it on camera about four hundred times, and, of course, shooting that picture with the baby for Ivory Snow. That was a trip—after they had selected my face from a few hundred, they needed the right baby to go with my looks. Then what? You guessed it. I had to have my picture taken with about four hundred babies. Wow!

So I was very successful for a kid from the sticks, a kid still in high school yet, and I dug New York like crazy, I mean I really loved it, and not only because it was my retreat from Connecticut.

I had always wanted to be an actress and I hated the fact that I could only go to the city for three or four hours and then have to come back home and be bright and fresh in geometry class the next day. Yecch, I hated math the most. And who could study or work as an actress that way? So I was getting a little uptight when I lucked out:

A phone call came. A guy I knew was the stand-in for George Segal on the filming of *The Owl and The Pussycat* and he asked me if I wanted to come down and see what a real movie set was like. Well, of course I did! I went down there, nosing around, kind of watching and listening because I believed one day I would be doing just that kind of work, and all of a sudden this guy says, "Hey, you."

"Me?"

"Yeah, you. You an actress?"

"Of course!" I said, flashing my biggest smile. The truth was I had taken only a few acting classes at the Neighborhood Playhouse and could hardly call myself an actress. But when a guy on a movie set with a cigar in his mouth asks, you immediately pretend you're Bette Davis.

I had no idea what he wanted or why he was asking, but I sure pretended I'd been on movie sets for years; it was old hat to me. He told me, "We're looking for a girl to play the part of Barney's girl. Can you stick around awhile?" *A while? I can stay for months if you like!* I said, "Sure," and sat down. So I hung around while they interviewed a few other girls, and then the guy said I had the part. We started that day and I worked on the film for about four or five whole days!

When I mention I was in *Pussy* the first question I get is always, "What was Barbra like?" Answer—I don't really know. I met her, yes, but I still don't know what to say about her. When people ask me about her I always grin and mutter something like, "She was very busy, you know?"

I ran up to her the first day of shooting and told her our birthdays were the same and she just looked at me and didn't seem too impressed. I talked to her a few more times—*to* her, not *with* her—and she wasn't very nice to me. She was constantly busy, doing this and that, making sure everything was correct, checking the lights and the makeup and doing what everyone in the place did after they had done it. She sure knew what she wanted. She also knew what she didn't want—me appearing too pretty or too naked, but I'll get to that later.

I did adore George Segal. He took me under his wing and gave me some good tips about the movie business and all. He was helpful and concerned, and although I didn't really tell him, I think he sensed that I was scared out of my skin and that it was the first film I'd ever worked on. He and my teacher at Neighborhood Playhouse were close friends, so that added another touch of closeness, and I'll always be grateful to him for explaining what was happening around me and translating the director's words into common language I could understand.

A few years later, I was able to compare the experience of working on a film like that to working on an X-film. In a legit motion picture, people are trying to be professional, but there are eyes watching you ... the actor and actress are supposed to play a big heavy love scene, but there are gaffers watching, makeup ladies watching, grips leering, coffee-runners running....

Wow. It's hard to do anything under those conditions, much less a love scene. My scene was very much that—very sexy and sensual. I was lying in bed and I remember looking up and seeing about a hundred people staring down at me. On an X-film, you have maybe five at the very most. You're trying to be serious and hard working in your scene, but there's all this stuff going on around you, all these things happening, all these people moving—I don't think an X-film could be made as a real Hollywood feature. Who could keep a hard-on while ninety-four heads are gobbling you up?

In an X-film, the atmosphere is relaxed, almost gentle, and very conductive to getting things accomplished. Only the director, cameraman, sound- and lightmen are there. You don't feel tense pressure. And that's good, because it's hard enough to perform sex in front of a camera, much less to have technicians standing around all over the place. It's a little easier on the girl because she doesn't have an erection to keep hard. But with the guy it's another story—if he loses his hard-on, if his prick goes *schlump!*, you have to cut and wait for him to get it back. The audience isn't going to go for a limp dick on screen. The girl is always more passive, things are always being done to her (take *Green Door's* Gloria, for example); the poor guy has to keep his cock hard and concentrate on fucking or eating the chick out or whatever he's doing, and then, to top it all off, reach an orgasm. And what if he's on the brink, just ready to come, and the third makeup lady with the powder puff in her hand farts or sneezes? *Zonk! Schlump!* You have to start all over again. That's why X-films don't have third makeup ladies and such time wasters (not to mention money wasters) all over the place. There are as few people as possible on an X-film set. So much money is wasted in a major motion picture.

Chuck worked on a lot of films—*PT109*, *The Happening*, the *Flipper* series, the *Gentle Ben* series—and he agrees with me about one thing: The actors (or many of them, at least) and people on the set are filled with the puritan ethic. The people who became stars twenty years ago think they're filled with openness and candor. But their heads stopped moving twenty years ago when they became famous or when the stagehands joined a union. They are the opposite of what they claim to be—uptight instead of liberal, inhibited instead of daring. Chuck has always said (and I think he's right) that sex films work because the people working on them don't have sexual hang-ups. Sex isn't an overpowering drive because they release it. And that's very unlike "legit" actors who sometimes allow sexual frustrations to ruin their films or their relationships with other actors, the crew, whomever.

Or producers. You'll be surprised to know there is no such thing as the "casting couch" in the X-film business. There is in legit films; everybody's horny but too uptight to be free with sex. Millions of dollars are wasted in legit films because of haphazard things, like the star walking off the set because she or he doesn't like the color of the lights, crap like that as opposed to X-films, where that kind of stuff just doesn't happen. Everyone working on an X-film knows it's being produced on a budget of forty grand and they realize that every second counts. A legit feature is made for millions and no one gives a damn. In a legit film, they shoot almost two hundred to one, that is two hundred feet of film for every one foot that's finally used in the finished print. In an X-film, it's about two to one, sometimes even one to one. X-film-makers can't take the chance of getting only half a can on someone. And everyone in an X-film knows that they're easily replaceable. Some of the big Hollywood stars should think that way.

Another interesting facet of X-films and their making is that many of the stars/directors/producers/crew are married to each other. Jason and Tina Russell are a perfect example. Sometimes you have a husband/star-wife/cameraman (or is it camerawoman?) situation. It emphasizes the point that no one can take the chance of being sexually uptight and jealous because no one can risk losing the footage because of someone getting pissed and walking off the set. Jason couldn't and wouldn't suddenly yell at Tina, "You're sucking his cock and liking it more than you like doing me!" It's ridiculous to think that such jealousy exists in X-films. The people are all doing their jobs and they're dedicated.

My experience on *The Owl and The Pussycat* is a good example of how uptight the atmosphere can be. You know what they made me wear in that "legit" film? I was supposed to be nude from the waist up, and that was pretty risqué four or five years ago, I mean people were going bananas over the "lewd" negligee Barbra wore in the big blow-up stills outside the theaters! Anyhow, Barbra didn't want me nude from the waist up 'cause she had a scene where she was supposed to be nude from the waist up—she didn't want any competition from the other girls in the film because she had a bed scene to play and her bed scene had to be the *shocker*! (if you know what I mean).

Some shocker.

Anyhow, they made me wear two body stockings, underwear, and a bra. Yes! To create the illusion that I was naked! Can you believe it? And the guy I was with had his underpants on. We were under the covers, sweating like crazy, giggling because the whole thing seemed so ludicrous, and I kept thinking, don't knock it; you're getting paid to do this.

I'd rather suck off a guy on a trapeze any day than roll around in a bed pretending to be nude while in fact I was bundled up like an Eskimo.

I believe in honesty in making a film.
The *Owl* scene wasn't honest.

When we were filming *The Resurrection of Eve*, years later, the guy who played Frank was rolling around in bed with me, sliding his cock in between my thighs, teasing me, and all of a sudden I flashed on filming *Owl* and how we sweated under those lights in those awful clothes with all those horny grips watching ... and I thought how different this was, how much easier it is to fuck on camera, to be natural, to do it honestly, the way people *really* do it in their bedroom. I played a legit bedroom scene and an X-bedroom scene, both saying to the audience, "Look, we're fucking!" and I'll go on record that the X-scene was by far easier, more exciting, more honest, and more fulfilling. And I'm speaking as an actress here, not as a sexy horny girl.

Speaking as a sexy horny girl, I'd have to make the same statement, however!

Yes, I really do believe in honesty in making a film. Simulated sex looks just like that, simulated sex. That's why *Deep Throat II* failed—it wasn't a real X-film, it was fake. That's why *Last Tango In Paris* disappointed me so. It was fake. They copped out. It's phony, the whole movie is phony, because it isn't real, it isn't honest. You sat there *knowing* the sex wasn't real. God, it was so dishonest it makes me scream! It could have been so wonderful! Real sex has a valid place in quality films. It shouldn't be flaunted. It should be used when necessary. Don't flaunt it, but don't hide it, for sure.

(I think it's interesting that Bertolucci recently stated that *Last Tango* was originally written for two men, that the

Maria Schneider role was actually supposed to be played by a boy. Now, had they done that and put in realistic sex, that would have been a gas, the most honest film ever made! But he [Bertolucci] said no one would finance it till he changed the young boy into a girl. A boyish girl to be sure, but a girl nonetheless.)

There's such pressure in big films. Maybe not in *Last Tango* because that was really a foreign film, but for sure in Hollywood numbers like *Owl*. I thought maybe my outlook was prejudiced because I worked on a Barbra Streisand film, and they say Barbra's films are the most pressurized of all, but Chuck says I'm not. I guess all big films are like that—dishonest. There's that big point of pleasing the star, holding her hand, petting her, cooing over her, taking care of her, making sure she's happy so she won't throw a fit to the tune of half a million bucks for that day's shooting. "All the bread's tied up in the star," Chuck says, "and that's all that's important, nothing else matters."

It was that way on *Pussycat*. And not only with Barbra. I mean everyone was afraid to tell anyone the truth, everyone skirted the issues, no one wanted a hassle. Sometimes hassles are great, you get over them, and things turn out for the better. I found it boring. Really boring. I always figure: *concentrate* on what you have to do, *do* it, and go home. If I have a scene to play, whether it's picking apples off a tree or licking a guy's balls, I do what I'm supposed to do and that's that. A Hollywood star who's used to being pampered would probably want the color of the apples changed because they clash with her hair, or maybe the slacks they gave her to wear in the scene cut into her ass too much so she wants a whole new wardrobe ... and if she's playing a cock-sucking scene (not very probable, I admit, but we can use our imaginations) she just may want the guy's dick to be an inch longer or a little more hair on his nuts. Ridiculous. But that's what they do. They'll shut down production for three days 'cause the star's bra straps are too tight. Christ!

I'm on screen for only a few moments in *Pussy* and we spent four days shooting that scene. There's the proof. What a waste (though I admit it was nice to be paid for four days' work). And here's the other side of the coin: Chuck started making porno films ("loops") in 1960 and they didn't even edit them. "They were so damned illegal, we couldn't *get* them edited!" he says. They shot them exactly as they were to be shown—no fucking around (no pun intended). Porno films back at that time were shot in nudist camps. You know, people with big bellies holding *Life* magazine in front of them, grinning at the big beautiful sun, playing volleyball so their tits and cocks were bouncing in the air but it was still legal and wholesome. "You kept the camera pointed between their legs and told them to jump," Chuck says laughingly, "and you hoped the jiggling tits didn't bug the censors." We've come a long way in a very short time.

Even hard-core magazines are new. "Hard core" back in the '60s meant nudist magazines, exposed pricks and cunts, and that was that. I remember my first year in high school, some of the guys were passing around a dirty book, a picture book of some kind, and all the girls wanted to see it. When we finally got hold of it, I was kind of surprised to see that the stuff all the guys were turning on to was tame. Pictures of naked people standing around in a park wasn't my idea of sexiness. I had better fantasies. But pictures turn people on, and those were the only kind of magazines you could get which showed cunts and cocks—only *Playboy* and a few others showed breasts. Exposed genitals excited guys, girls too, and even though they were tame compared with the hard-core fuckbooks of today, those nudist magazines were good jack-off material when I was in high school. Unless you were lucky enough to have a father or an older brother with a cache of French porno hidden at the back of his closet (which I didn't, unfortunately). Not many of our fathers were that liberated. And we all were horny kids.

Thank God for masturbation.

I always masturbated a lot, from the time I was very small. It's a very healthy thing. *Very!* I remember feeling extremely guilty about it at one time, but I don't anymore and as I get older, I do it more and more. I think it's how you make yourself supersensitive, really supersensual. The more you sensitize your body, the more it's going to react to stimulation, whether it's a guy's finger in there or a girl's tongue or a Coke bottle.

I think it's so crazy and stupid when I hear of women who find out their husband or lover jerked off in the bathroom one morning and they go through this "Am I not pleasing him enough?" trip. That's bullshit. I think it's great when people jerk off. "Oh, weep for me! He has to go proud his meat in the bathroom when he could be giving it to me. Oh, but what's happening to our relationship?" That's just crazy! Masturbation is terrific, alone or with someone else. I mean people should respect each other's privacy-fantasy trip, doing it while looking at yourself in the mirror or while sitting on the toilet … why not act out your fantasies? Whatever turns you on. If we have the power to reach an orgasm alone, without a partner, what's wrong with that?

Just the fact that we're blessed with it, as human beings, must mean we were meant to masturbate, right?

I'm a masturbation freak. I think it's one of the best things in the world. Some people need sex more than others and I happen to be one of them. I love it. Chuck has often said that one of the reasons I come off the way I do on screen is because I look as though I'm enjoying what I'm doing, and the fact is I do. "Linda," he says, "was very uptight about sex at first, when she first began making films, and it took a lot of work to get her to the point where she loved it, but she never got to love it as Marilyn loves it." I think that's because I got to love it long before I had the slightest idea I'd be doing it on camera one day.

I don't know how I compare with Linda and I don't really care to have people saying one of us is the best, because we're all different, Linda, Georgina, Tina, me. All I know is that I'm truthful in those films—I really, honestly, truly (criss-cross my heart again) love what's happening on the screen at any given moment, whether I'm fucking up a storm or vacuuming the floor. And I think that's what acting is all about, being honest is what you're doing. "Marilyn can reach past the camera," Chuck once told an interviewer, "and that's what most porno people can't do." I see that as only one man's opinion, Marilyn as seen through one man's eyes, that I'm a good actress. But that man is very important to me, and very honest with me—he's always first my biggest critic, then my fan. So I take his words as a challenge and want to prove them in the future.

4

Making a Woman, The "Pussy Tour" and San Francisco

Pornography is changing people's attitudes, forcing them to think in new directions, forcing them to open up. I think the laws against pornography, as the laws against marijuana, will change; porno laws will die faster than laws against grass, however. We still have the preoccupation with "the terrors of marijuana," where we have less and less censorship. I think people should be able to see whatever they choose to see, especially if they're paying their hard-earned money to do it.

And I think people should be able to smoke grass if they want to. I can't say anything beyond that because I haven't tried any other drugs and don't want to. They frighten me and I'm happy the way I am. I don't need them. I get high on people, sex, and sometimes grass, and that's high enough. That's already in the clouds. I get high on performing and then I'm in outer space.

The first time I smoked grass was in high school, when I was about sixteen. I was a big dud. I didn't turn on; I didn't feel a thing. A girl told me to come to her car with her and we smoked that weed I'd heard so much about, and thought, "This is what everyone's so nuts about?"

I think I must have smoked a few more times while I was in high school, but it never did much for me. Either we didn't have good dope in Westport (Dealers, head for Connecticut—they're dying for some good stuff up there!) or I just wasn't into it. At that time, I'd take a can of beer any day.

My first experience with getting high on grass has a great deal to do with another first experience in my life—my first lesbian affair.

We can thank Clairol for the start of that. Funny how all these famous products have something to do with my personal life! Anyway, I got a Clairol commercial shortly after *Pussy*, for one of their products, called Kindness, a hair conditioner. I was one of six chicks who said, "We don't need Kindness." I had to wear an enormous frazzled wig down to my rear and I could barely stand up under the weight of it. Then a chick came out and said, "I need Kindness," and she looked great and her hair was beautiful and so on. We must have done it about three hundred times and we were beat by the time the shooting was finished.

I changed clothes and sat down in a waiting room in the studio for a few minutes—I think I was waiting to find out if they needed us again the next day or something like that. Then I noticed a woman looking at me. She reminded me of Sophia Loren, very strong, very feminine, and she had a dynamite body, big boobs, and long legs. I had seen many beautiful women in my life but there was something special about her. I didn't know what it was but I couldn't take my eyes off her.

She came over to me and told me it was nice to see me again. I didn't know what she meant. I didn't remember having met her, and I thought I would have. She explained that we'd made a commercial together with a lot of other people and I just hadn't noticed her. But she had noticed me. She asked if I wanted a ride home and I told her yes, sure. I'd just gotten my own apartment in New York (well, I had a roommate, but she wasn't there a lot of the time, which I didn't mind) and realized that cabs were very expensive and subways too hot and crowded. So a ride in a real car seemed like a treat.

Her name was Helen and she was thirty-five years old. I felt at ease with her immediately and we found that we could talk with each other about serious things without being uptight. It seemed as though we'd known each other for years and years.

We stopped on the way to my place to pick up her boyfriend. She had been married, had a child, divorced, and now lived with her son and spent a lot of time with her boyfriend. I liked him too, and I asked if they wanted to come up to my apartment for coffee, and they did.

And that's when they offered me some grass. Well, I laughed and told them it hadn't done anything for me in the past, but they said it was good stuff and urged me to try it anyway. So I did.

Zonk!

I was flying in about five minutes. Well, no, not really flying, but very calm and collected (which rarely happened after a hectic day's shooting) and turned on sexually, which I kept from them. We laughed and talked and they said, "See, it does work for you!" and I nodded and giggled. It did. It was an entirely new experience for me. I figured, Aha! Now I know what to do to keep my nerves in shape while being a model!

When they left, I fell to the bed and closed my eyes and had the best sleep I'd had in years.

And then I saw Helen again. She called and asked if I'd like to have lunch with her, and we met in a little restaurant on Third Avenue and spent hours talking. We didn't do much eating or drinking but we sure talked a lot. And our talk included sex, of course. It was very general, except for my telling her the story of the loss of my virginity on that rainy night, and then she asked me if I had ever made it with another girl.

"No."

"Have you ever wanted to?"

I would have said no to that too, had she been any person other than who she was. I told her the truth. In high school, I had become friendly with a girl who had recently moved to town. I think that's why I had the nerve to ask Helen what I eventually asked her—because I hadn't grown up with her and didn't know a whole lot about her.

One night this girl came to my house and we went out for a walk, as we often did, talking about boys and classes and dreams. She encouraged me, told me I'd make a great model and actress, and I gave her a shoulder to cry on because she was having trouble at home, her parents weren't getting along. We gave each other strength. Well, that night we felt extremely close to each other and we held hands. I think at one point we even hugged. Then we came back to my house and sat on the patio long past the time the rest of my family had gone to sleep. There was a kind of restlessness in both of us that night which we couldn't explain then. It was sexual; there was no doubt about it. We couldn't bear to part. But we couldn't bear to be honest enough to go to bed together either.

Finally, she said something about how she had heard that many of the guys at school thought I "put out," and I told her I loved them thinking that because it really wasn't true. I'd only had a few experiences by then, beginning with the disaster in the rain. She said she envied me because she was still a virgin and hated it. Then I asked if she had ever balled with another chick. I didn't put it quite so bluntly, but that was what I was basically asking.

She didn't tighten up at all. "No, I haven't," she said.

Then I asked the biggie, and I almost shocked myself by saying it. "Would you like to do it with me?"

There was no answer. I think we sat there for five or six embarrassing minutes, wondering what to say, how to change the subject, how to continue....

Finally, I said, "I guess I didn't mean that. I just thought for a second it would be fun to see what it's like."

"Yes," she said softly, "maybe it would be ... sometime."

The "sometime" meant "certainly not now" and that was that. I never brought it up again and we were never again as close as we had been that night.

And here I was, sitting in a restaurant with Helen, telling her about the same conversation that was taking place between us. Helen was asking me the questions I had asked my girlfriend in high school. Helen said, "She wasn't ready for it then."

"Neither was I, I don't think," I replied.

"Are you now?"

I looked into her big brown knowledgeable eyes and said, "I'm not sure." But I knew damn well that she knew the truth—I was ready and I wanted it to be with her.

But we didn't go any further than that. I told her I'd call her soon and we said goodbye in front of the restaurant and just before she got into a cab, she gave me a little kiss on the cheek. I felt a surge of excitement. I waved as she drove away and for the rest of the day I couldn't forget what that kiss had done to me.

I'd told her I would call. So I did, that night. That very night. She was surprised to hear from me so soon, she said, but I think she was hoping I'd call, or kind of expecting me to. We talked gibberish for a few minutes and then I said that I'd thought about it and I felt I was ready.

"I think I am too," she said.

"It could be fun, I imagine," I said, shaking and sweating the way I did the first time a boy tried to get me to rest my hand between his legs.

"Yes, great fun, and very pleasing also," Helen said softly. "Would you like to make love to me?"

"Um, I guess ... yeah, I would."

And we set a night; we'd give it a try.

So I showed up on the appointed night, trembling but very anxious. It was so unknown, the way New York had seemed when I first started modeling, the way anything you haven't done or experienced seems—enticing. But I was a bit surprised when her boyfriend opened the door. I thought he had maybe dropped in for a few minutes or something, but after a while, I realized that he was planning on staying the night.

And that he knew what Helen and I had planned.

That threw me. It was a little like my first experience with the football player—everything it had been cracked up to be suddenly went down the drain. I had pictured a warm bed and violins playing, and instead I got a car sinking into the mud, my foot in a horn, a shift knob between my legs, and the sound of rain hitting metal. I pictured my first sexual experience with another woman happening out in the country, by a brook or stream, doing it in the grass under the sun. Instead, I got a small apartment on the East Side, a baby sleeping in the next room, and a guy sitting in the corner watching us, jerking off. Oh, yes. That's how it ended up.

They had a box of grass sitting on the coffee table, a big box of grass, and I was happy to see it because I knew it would help soothe my nerves and probably get me to accept her boyfriend being there. You know, it was interesting that they didn't strike me as the kind of people who smoke grass. He was a businessman, like my father, and she was a model, but a very high-fashion model. I thought then that only hip young people smoked grass.

So they got out a pipe and we started to smoke and I soon realized she was more nervous than I was. "Hey, this is cool," her boyfriend would say, and she'd take his hand, and it dawned on me that it was her first time too—or, rather, it was going to be. Wow. My first fuck with a guy turns out to be a virgin, and now my first experience with another chick turns out the same way. But she had a lot more class than the football player, and after we started there was no stopping her.

I began feeling very stoned and I kind of fell back on some pillows and she bent over and kissed me lightly on the lips. I felt that surge of pleasure that I'd experienced on the street when she'd kissed me. So I ran my fingers through her hair and smiled, and she kissed me again and this time I opened my lips and our tongues met. I heard a sound and glanced across the table. Her boyfriend was unfastening his belt. I started to pull away because I didn't want anything to do with him, although he was a very nice guy, but she stopped me and said, "He's just going to watch, honey." And her eyes put me at ease again and I fell into her arms and we started making love.

Our clothes came off slowly and we kissed every part of each other's bodies. I found myself wishing I'd forced that girl in high school into doing it that night—I realized how much I had been missing. Sex with guys was wonderful, but it was only half of the coin. I wanted both sides and I found myself loving it. I was fascinated with the idea of feeling and kissing and loving a body just like mine only belonging to someone else. When people ask me why I'm bisexual or what's the magic of homosexuality, lesbianism, or bisexuality, I tell them just that—that making love to someone who is exactly like you is a trip like no other. Who knows better how to please a woman physically than another woman, who has the same body and knows what pleases her? Guys have often told me that girls give great head but they haven't found one who's as good as another guy. That's because another guy knows how a blow job feels when he gets one, so he can translate that into action when he gives one himself. I'm not saying that's true in every case or even that it's the best. I'm only saying that everyone should try it and see. I think people should have a completely well-rounded sex life. They should be able to get it on with anyone they're attracted to, the opposite sex or their own.

Helen's body was as beautiful nude as it was clothed. Her breasts were large and firm and her pussy was so hairy and soft, so feminine, and so damp—so much like mine, I thought, and that turned me on. I had often masturbated in front of a mirror, looking at myself. I think everyone does that sometime in their life, masturbate while looking at themselves, getting off on themselves, and I think it's very healthy. So now, I was with a woman—someone who had a body just like mine!

She kissed me on the lips and then slid her tongue into my mouth and I let her hands run all over me, pinching my nipples and gently tickling my pussy. Her boyfriend sat in the corner of the room, playing with himself, just watching in breathless fascination. Then she moved her mouth down, kissed my breasts, and finally took my nipples in her lips. I really grooved on it, and I think she sucked on my breasts for about twenty minutes.

Then she asked if I wanted to go to the bedroom, and I was so turned on, I would have gone anywhere.

So Helen let me stretch out on the bed and she knelt next to me, just staring at me, smiling, looking at my body. I think she felt much the same as I felt; being so fascinated with a body so much like hers. She put her head between my legs and kissed my pussy lips and I purred like a cat and her boyfriend came into the room and stood in the corner, watching, pulling on his cock, his eyes red, his face excited. He didn't come near us. He just stood there and watched—it must have been a trip for him.

We made love nearly all night. She did things to me that I'd never dreamed of having done, the way she moved her tongue in my pussy, tickling my clitoris, rubbing her fingers over my stomach and breasts. And she was so gentle, so loving. A little scared at times—I could feel her tremble—but the excitement won out.

We held each other in that bed, tightly, running our fingers down each other's backs, feeling our thighs locking together as our pussies rubbed each other, as our tits pressed between us. We rolled around and finally twisted our bodies around in such a way that I was facing her cunt and she was facing mine. I hesitated for a moment because I had never before had my face so close to another girl's pussy, but as I felt Helen's tongue sliding up my own cunt I moved my lips to hers and kissed her lovingly, almost as though I were thanking her for giving me such pleasure. I wrapped my arms around her rounded ass and held her tight, pressing her warmth to my face, making love to her the way she was making love to me. I heard her boyfriend let out a short, muffled gasp, and I turned my head and saw sperm shooting from the tip of his cock. He sank to the floor, looking dazed, his prick limp in his hand. He was worn out.

Then Helen got up from the bed, but I hadn't climaxed and I didn't want to stop making love. She wasn't going far, I soon found out. She got her dildo out of a drawer and knelt between my spread thighs and fucked me with it. It was just like a guy's cock, just like a hand masturbating me, but it was a piece of plastic that looked like a penis but was in reality an extension of this woman's desires and passions—she wanted to enter me, to fuck me, but she had no penis, so she used an artificial one and the fucking was in her mind. And it felt so good! Seeing her sliding that long fake cock in and out of my pussy turned her boyfriend on again, and he opened his eyes and his cock jerked back to attention. He whacked off some more while Helen worked the dildo on me and then her boyfriend said, "Helen, use your vibrator."

Helen listened to him. And I was glad, because she had a terrific vibrator, almost the size of the dildo she had been using, and it stimulated me even more. We took turns working it on each other, giggling like two schoolgirls, sliding the vibrator into each other, watching it and feeling it and grooving it. That was the first time in my life that I'd ever used one, and I liked it so much that I ran out the very next day and bought one of my own.

Oh, it was an amazing night. I had a tremendous orgasm when Helen slid the vibrator all the way up me and kissed me hard on the lips at the same time, pressing her big rough nipples into my flesh. She had an orgasm when I kissed her and tickled her clitoris with my fingertips. Her boyfriend watched and came again and moaned as a second load of cream poured down his hand.

The best thing about the night, the thing that was most amazing, sexually, and what I recall best, is the way Helen performed cunnilingus on me, the way she ate my pussy. I realized at the time that I was no longer the sheltered schoolgirl, no more the giggle-girl, no more the naive daughter. I mean by now I had learned how to take a guy's cock in my mouth and a few boys I'd been with had attempted to eat me (by that I mean they weren't very good at it). But I envied her having a boyfriend, having an old man. Because then I didn't have one, and I was lonely.

Now I do have one and it's wonderful because I can get it on with a woman and not feel lonely later. Girls do turn me on, a lot. That ravishment by the chicks in *Green Door* wasn't all acting, believe me—I loved it! I like very feminine, voluptuous chicks, usually with big breasts, as opposed to very butch women.

Well, that's not entirely true. A few months ago, Chuck and I were on an Amtrack going somewhere for a personal appearance thing and I noticed a very beautiful woman who looked like a very beautiful man. I said, "Chuck, look at that chick over there, she looks like a guy, she's dressed like a guy." He looked at her and nodded. Then I found myself saying, "I wonder what it would be like to ball her?" And then Chuck and I broke up, giggling. People must often think we're crazy, because we start laughing and can't stop. We have so much fun together and we share little secrets and private jokes. A chick will come up to me and ask me for my autograph and as I'm signing it I glance at Chuck and he reads my mind (knowing I'm thinking what it would be like to get it on with her) and we break up in laughter and the girl thinks I'm totally freaked out. Oh well.

I still haven't made it with a butch chick. I still wonder what it would be like. I guess you wouldn't have to make any role decision—if she's wearing hiking boots it's made for you already, no consultation necessary! Maybe I'll try it sometime. I like new experiences. And if they turn out to be bummers, okay. At least you tried, right?

Because I've always been very open about bisexuality. I'm often asked if I have a lot of gay friends. Gay guys, yes. Bisexuals, yes. Strictly lesbian chicks, no. I don't know why that is. I think with many strictly gay girls that the domination instinct is so strong that it carries over from bed into everyday life, never allowing another's opinion or idea to enter the conversation. And I find that boring. But that's making a big generalization. I guess maybe I just haven't met enough chicks who are strictly lesbian—and I don't think there are that many. Many of the few out-and-out dykes I've met put me down because I'm not submissive enough. I like to do everything, sexually, ball men and women, and they don't seem to like that; they find that too strong, too dominant.

Speaking of dominant dykes, Chuck has a story he like to tell which I think is pretty funny. He played football in college and he weighed about 190 pounds and he had a friend who was about six-foot-four and weighed 260 pounds. He played tackle. And they went into a lesbian bar one night, started drinking beer, pinching the barmaid on the ass. And the chick really dug it. She was probably bisexual and she was turning on to Chuck's friend, who was a big, good-looking guy.

Right about closing time, he grabbed her by the arm and said, "My friend and I'll be out by the car waiting for you…." And then Chuck heard this mighty roar and he turned to see the bull dyke who ran the place leap over the bar like Tarzan, lift a beer can into the air—a full one, a heavy one, not an empty aluminum can—and smash it into his pal's face! It knocked him off the stool and onto the floor and she jumped on top of him and started beating the shit out of him. So Chuck grabbed her and pulled her off his pal, then hauled off and slugged her in the jaw. Then they got the hell out of there.

Well, the cops found them and they were really worried because they were two football players from the University of Miami and they were up for aggravated assault for punching out a chick. They thought, oh fuck, they'd never win. Even their attorney said they didn't have a chance. The dyke would waltz into the courtroom looking like Greta Garbo or Jean Harlow and that would finish them right there. Men don't hit women, not even in Florida in a lesbian bar.

So the court date came and they were all assembled and Chuck and his buddy were dressed in cardigan sweaters and slacks, looking very boyish and all-American, worried and sweating. Then the door opened and in she walked, like a truck driver. She was wearing a man's suit, a tie, men's shoes, and to top it all off she carried a big, gold-knobbed walking stick. Only thing missing was the cigar. Well, they couldn't believe it. Chuck and his friend looked like little kids next to the Everglades Bruiser. The judge said something like, "Looks like a case of a couple of the boys fighting it out in a bar to me," and dismissed the case. Chuck says she was shouting obscenities and rapping her walking stick on the judge's bench even as the courtroom was emptying.

I haven't been in more than three dyke bars in my life, so maybe this is prejudiced, but I found all three of them to be lacking in humor. No one was having any fun; the atmosphere seemed oppressed. And the reason I haven't been in more than three is that I have no desire to go to any because those three turned me off so.

I love gay bars, on the other hand. Especially dancing ones, which are springing up all over the country. I think they're the best places to dance and have a good time. You can be yourself and have fun. San Francisco had some great bars like that when I lived there (I'm sure it still does) and I could go there with another chick and not feel threatened by anyone, man or woman; you could relax or rap or dance or anything. And I'm very used to gay men—some very masculine, some very swishy—because I've known them ever since I started getting into modeling and show business in New York. I find them interesting, full of humor, kind and considerate, and usually quite talented—and if they turn out otherwise, turn out to be the "depressed homosexual" and on that heavy trip, I just walk away. The old saying "some of my best friends are gay" is really very true in my case. What counts first is that they're my friends; their sexuality comes second to that. They're not my friends because they're gay, they're my friends because they're good people, people I care about and have a good time with.

Anyway, that feeling of being alone that I'd felt after I left Helen that night never really left me completely till I met Douglas Chapin. And how I got to San Francisco, met, and married him is quite another story. It all happened because of—again—*Pussycat.*

Pussy was set to open and a tour had been arranged but Barbra wasn't going to do it and neither was George Segal. I don't know if they couldn't or wouldn't, but it didn't matter—they needed someone from the picture to attend the openings.

Guess who got asked? Yes, Marilyn Briggs. And Roz Kelly, the girl who plays the hooker in the bookstore in the movie. Twentieth Century-Fox asked us to publicize the film at their expense, and it was crazier for me than for Roz because my name didn't even appear in the credits. It was stupid. Who wants to see someone who has a walk-on part in the film being interviewed at the premiere? But who was I to question such stupidity? It meant a free trip to California, a place I had never been to but had dreamed of visiting. A place that would change my life.

So we had our plane tickets, reservations at the Beverly Wilshire in Los Angeles and the Fairmont in San Francisco, and carte blanche to charge anything and everything at Twentieth Century-Fox. Wow. Far out. It was better than beating the streets as a model in Manhattan.

Los Angeles was fun, mainly because I got to know some people at Fox, and finally met Ray Stark, who produced *Pussy*, and since I was on the *Pussy* tour, we became friends. He sent me to a couple of readings for other pictures, but I was too this or too that and nothing worked out. But I hadn't counted on becoming a movie star because of the tour; I mean, the first-class plane ride was thrilling enough!

I had built quite an image of Los Angeles in my mind, subtropical, oranges and lemons growing on every tree, clear and beautiful. I remember landing in the smog and then looking up outside the airport to see exactly the same sky I'd left in New York—gray. So things like roses in the hotel room and free bottles of champagne helped make up for the wreck of my L. A. dream.

Roz and I made appearances at the theater where *Pussy* opened, and a few other places around town, out to dinner and a few radio and TV shows, parties, photo sessions, all that stuff. We were supposed to be there for about two weeks but after a week we realized that there really was nothing to do there and we asked if we could go up to San Francisco sooner than planned. They said sure and off we went.

And I fell in love with a town for the first time in my life. "I left my heart in San Francisco..." La la la. It's true. It can steal your heart. It's unlike any city in this country. It's completely unique. Roz and I did the tour thing, the appearances for *Pussy*, the interviews, and all, but when that was over I decided to stick around for a few more weeks. I had my plane ticket back, so that was secure, and some friends of mine had a big house and a lot of little cabins up in the mountains north of San Francisco, in Calistoga, just above Napa, and I went up there for a kind of vacation-after-the-vacation. It was beautiful—woods and animals and blue skies. I wanted to stay a lifetime.

Instead, I went back to New York.

Ugh. Rat race. Everyone seemed to be trapped and I didn't want that to happen to me. I went back to my apartment (my roommate was gone again) and found myself sitting there, ticked off that I could see black air outside the window, saying, "I left California for this?" Even Los Angeles regained its dream image when I compared it to New York. I suddenly felt I had found my niche. I proclaimed I was a Californian.

I started packing immediately.

It wasn't hard to leave. I had made no really close friendships that I'd have to break. Nothing much was happening with my career. I didn't really feel I belonged to anything or anyone. I was in a kind of limbo. Nothing compared with California, the people, the climate... I even thought there was more theater, better theater, in San Francisco, and I deluded myself into thinking that it would be easier to break into than New York theater. So I got out. Goodbye cockroaches, hello sunshine!

I borrowed my parents' car, piled all my stuff into it, and drove back to Westport. Then I got a drive-away car and headed cross-country, Route 66 all the way, through the desert, the mountains—it was dynamite! I'd never done anything like it before. I felt so free and untrapped and sure of the future.

I wound up in Laguna Beach, which was the California of my early dreams: beautiful skies, the blue Pacific, the unhurried life, nice people, lots of good vibes; just the way I'd pictured it back in Connecticut. Laguna was nice but nothing happens there and it was time to start thinking about making some money on which to live. It's much easier to survive in California than in New York. Heck, if you don't have an apartment, sleep on the beach. Besides, I was longing for San Francisco and the world of theater.

And so I moved to the City by the Bay.

I was a real Californian.

I cut my hair real short, married a mechanic who played the bagpipes, and became the star of a pornographic movie. Life changes when you become a real Californian.

5

Doug, Ivory Snow's Essence of Purity, and Porno Queen All in the Same Week!

Cutting my hair was the first real trauma. I don't know why I did it. I guess because I wanted to change everything, to start anew, to leave the old Marilyn Briggs behind. Cutting your hair changes the way you walk, the way you talk, feel, act, think—it's really something. So I did it, and then I set out to conquer San Francisco. I was worldly; I was seasoned, right? Hell, I'd come from a very successful modeling career in New York City, I'd done a promotional tour for a major film, I'd had a lesbian affair and lived to tell about it, I'd driven across America all by myself!

I was naive.

San Francisco theater was a closed circle; there was no way of penetrating it short of being born into it or marrying into it, neither of which I did. I found it terribly frustrating, worse than going from modeling agency to modeling agency in New York. To my dismay, I found that San Francisco is not a good place for an actress to look for work. I tried dance groups, little theaters, big theaters, singing groups, anything

I could possibly be right for, and I felt like a high school girl trying to break into someone else's clique. It was families and communes and no outsiders were allowed.

So the string of odd jobs came along. I worked in an organic restaurant, slinging vegetables instead of hash, which was very earthy and natural but far from what I wanted to do in life. I was the hostess (a pretentious title for nothing more than a waitress who doesn't carry dishes) at some dump for a while, and then, when money was really tight, I did topless/bottomless dancing in another dump. Anything to stay alive, to keep the body in shape, because even though times were rough I had ambition and plans for the future. I just didn't know how they were going to work out, what was going to turn the key to open the door to a career. If someone had said sucking cock on screen would do it, I would have laughed at him and then slapped him. Funny how things turn out.

And funny how people pop up now and then, here and there, and how they change your life. I don't think there will ever be a situation in my life as unique as my meeting Doug for the first time. Nothing that ridiculous could ever happen again.

I was walking down the street one day, feeling a bit lonely I guess, and suddenly I heard this strange music. You hear lots of music on the streets of San Francisco, flutes and violins, maybe even a tuba now and then, or something someone's made from an old washtub. But this music was distinctly different and yet it was familiar. Bagpipes. My parents are English and Scottish, in fact my mother's parents were born in Scotland, so I was raised with "bagpipes in the background."

So I said, "Oh, wow, that sounds really nice," and I wondered if someone had on a record or if someone near me was carrying a radio or something ... but no. As I neared the corner, it got louder and louder. Then, as I turned the corner, I saw him. A great-looking young guy sitting on the cement playing the bagpipes. It knocked me out!

"Sounds great," I said, or something equally inane, and I hung out there for a while, standing around. I even gave him some money!

I'd always heard that crap about two people being in the right place at the right time, and suddenly it wasn't crap. We dug each other. He stopped playing long enough to tell me that his name was Doug and invited me home with him. So I went home with him. And stayed for two years.

I fell in love. It's as pure and simple as that, if falling in love ever can be pure and simple. And Doug fell in love with me. That first day in his apartment, we weren't nervous at all, as I'd been in all the sexual affairs I'd had previously. I mean I would always wonder what the guy was going to be like, if we would hit it off, if he'd like me—all that junk. With Doug it didn't matter. I wasn't scared. I didn't wonder what he was going to be like; I knew. He was going to be great. And he was. It was bliss. Making love with him was like nothing I'd ever done, and we did it nonstop for days.

I was living with some friends at the time I met him, and they were just moving out of their apartment and I had to find a place to go, so it was perfect. I moved in with Doug. And we lived together for a year before we decided to get married.

I think that year was the best time we had together. We were in love, really in love, faithful to each other, happy, thinking that the world was beautiful. I've changed a lot since then and it would be easy to look back on it and say it was a mistake and I shouldn't have done it. But it wasn't a mistake, not at that time. It was something I needed, a time I had to go through, a piece of my lifetime in which I had to grow and think and decide what kind of future I really wanted, and a time to be happy. So I can't let the fact that our marriage finally ended and the fact that I made some mistakes in my marriage (such as never forcing Doug to get a job) cloud what really was there that first year, and much of the second too.

Doug was (and is) a nice guy. That's what everyone says about him. Everyone likes him so much, they find it hard to tell him that he has any faults. I didn't tell him he had any faults. He worked on cars once in a while and he played the bagpipes and I loved him. No faults. And our sex life was terrific. Doug's cock was always hard, he was always horny, and I was always ready for it. A lot of people have said, "Man, 'cause she's a porno star, she must have been a real ballbuster. That poor jerk she was married to!"

Ballbuster, bullshit. Everyone forgets I hadn't even had the thought to make a porno film when I met Doug, and even after I made *Green Door* and *Eve,* we had a terrific sex life. We fucked like crazy because we were young and horny. Sex is a normal desire, a great one, the best we have. But for all those silly ideas that I'd come home from shooting and rape poor Douglas, that's just ridiculous. I like pleasing a man, making him happy. Especially my man. And Doug was my man. I was always ready to give him head, I mean, I could suck on his cock for hours. But if he wanted to do something else, fine with me—pleasing him was the important thing. People have visions of my swinging on a vine, pouncing on him, and ordering him to fuck me. I did what would make

Doug the happiest; that's the kind of woman I am. If I'm getting it on, whether with a girl or a guy, I always want to please them. Their satisfaction comes first. And I get great pleasure from it.

Anyway, that first year was super. We were like little kids, flower children grown up, bopping around the hills of San Francisco, spending a lot of time in bed, enjoying living. Then one day we joked about getting married. We said something like, "We'll get married and have a house in the suburbs and pass out grass to the straights down the street." It was silly talk but suddenly we found ourselves feeling committed to it. All of a sudden, we really wanted to be legally married. (We did get that house in the 'burbs, but we never did pass out grass to the neighbors!)

I called my mother. "Hi, mom. I'm gonna marry a bagpipe player."

Silence.

"Mom, you there?" I guess mothers always want their daughters to say, "I'm in love with a lawyer." A doctor. A minister, even. Something respectable, something acceptable. I told my parents I was marrying a *bagpipe player*. "Does he play professionally, Marilyn?"

Sure, mom, he's first chair in the San Francisco Symphony's bagpipe section.

Well, they weren't all that shocked. By then they were beginning to realize their little girl was a little screwball. They were beginning to accept the fact that I was different and would be doing things differently for the rest of my life.

At first, my parents fought it, for about a week. They were understandably concerned and wanted the best for me, but they also realized that I was going to do it anyway, so they figured they'd better give me their "blessing," as it is called. My God, Doug and I had lived together, fucking every night, for a year, what was the difference now? We were making our bedroom frolics legal, that's what we were doing. Now my parents could tell their friends who slept with Marilyn. Marilyn's husband.

The wedding was a trip; it was beautiful. I wanted it to be held outdoors, in the forest. The ceremony was held on Mount Tamalpais, California, overlooking the ocean. My parents came out for it, my brother and sister, all our friends. We took off our shoes and danced in the grass. It really was beautiful. Then we had a reception down at a lodge, where some friends cooked a big meal and we all had a good time.

But good times are balanced by bad times. Doug and I didn't have a whole lot of money and I was always searching the ads for something for an actress to do. And then the day came which I've already told you about, the day I found the Mitchell brothers' ad. And the *Green Door* came into our lives.

Even before I answered the Mitchell brothers' ad in the *Chronicle* in 1971, I was beginning to wonder when Douglas was going to do something. He worked on cars once in a while, when the spirit moved him, and played pipes on the street when he felt like it, but there was no income and we had to live. We had to keep the dog fed. We had to pay rent. So I went out and kept going through my series of odd jobs until the films came along. And though I was happy with Doug, happy in bed and happy on an intellectual level, I really wished he'd get his ass in gear and decide what to do with his life. He never could make up his mind. He's that kind of person, a born follower, and though I didn't realize it then, I needed a man who was a leader.

After *Green Door* opened and the Ivory Snow thing hit, Doug seemed even more content to stay home and let me go out and bring in the bread. When I was doing a publicity thing for *Green Door,* just before it opened in San Francisco and Los Angeles, Doug and I moved to Walnut Creek, that suburb we had joked about, and we loved our little house and new lifestyle. It would bore me later, but for about a year it was so different we found it interesting.

I guess the most interesting thing that happened when we lived in Walnut Creek was the way I discovered my face on the Ivory Snow box....

Someone once said to me, "How could you dare to do two such diametrically opposed things as the Ivory Snow box and porno film at the same time?" My answer is: first of all, it's easy, and secondly, it's fun. There was nothing in my contract with Procter & Gamble that said I couldn't do dirty movies. In fact, I thought they had forgotten all about me. I figured they'd gotten another girl or something and my face would never be on the box. But when it did show up it couldn't have happened at a better time.

Two years before the soap boxes with my face appeared on the supermarket shelves I'd gone to a regular casting call. It was for a new face for the Ivory Snow box, a "pure face," as they called it. I figured I was pure enough, so I went, but it was no big deal, it was just another call. They wanted someone new because the same woman's face had been on the box for about twelve years and she was beginning to look a bit dated. Just as Mamie Eisenhower is not the symbol of the '70s, this chick on the Ivory Snow box was not your essence of the young mother of today. They wanted the "now" generation housewife and mother. And so they took a lot of test shots with a lot of girls, and then took more shots of us holding babies, and finally they told me I was the one. I was surprised and very happy, of course, and I knew I'd make some nice money.

Well, after they decided on my face they needed to decide on a baby's face, and I think I held a hundred screaming, crying, wet-diapered babies, and another hundred smiling, cooing, laughing babies. I love babies, want my own someday, but I didn't love them enough to enjoy sitting through all those photo sessions. Hell, Marilyn, you're getting paid for this, this is what modeling's all about....

Sometimes I'd begin to think my dad was right, that the world of modeling was pure insanity and masochism.

But I stuck it out and it was the biggest stroke of luck I've had in my life, though I wasn't about to realize that till two years later in a supermarket in Walnut Creek, California.

They finally chose a baby. It had the right face, but red hair, and we were both supposed to be blondes. And we're blonde on the box. You figure it out. Sounds more like a Clairol ad, right?

So I did the thing for Procter & Gamble and went on my merry way. Then the week *Green Door* opened in San Francisco I went to the supermarket to get something for dinner. Every now and then when I had been in a store I'd check out the soap boxes, just for the heck of it, and there she was, every time, the same chick from twelve years ago. I really didn't think I'd ever be on the box, but I kept looking anyhow. Then that evening—we were having a barbecue, I think—I was in the store getting last-minute things we needed, I took my usual glance at the soap section and I stood there and said, "Is that me?" I think I giggled like crazy because I'd never seen the picture and I wasn't sure it really was me at first. But it was. And that red-headed baby was now a blonde, too! Was it Clairol? I'll never know.

And the funny thing was, I didn't have enough money with me to buy a box, I had to come back in the morning. And when I returned to the store in the morning (the clerk thought I was opening up a laundry because I bought four boxes and nothing else). I found a residual check from Procter & Gamble in the mailbox, informing me that they had used my picture and here was the money due me. I had been paid a flat fee when the photos were taken, with a clause in the contract that should it be used on the box someday I would be paid another thousand dollars.

So Doug and I were a thousand bucks richer.

And I was about a million dollars richer in publicity.

Fate, stroke of luck, coincidence, irony, call it whatever you wish, it was the best thing that could have happened to me. It wasn't a case of my manager (I really didn't have one; Chuck hadn't entered my life as yet and the Mitchell brothers were acting in that capacity) going to Procter & Gamble and saying, "Hey, Mr. Procter and Mr. Gamble, I'll give you fifty million dollars if you put Marilyn's picture on your soap boxes." It just happened, and the timing was right.

At first, Doug and I were worried about what would happen. I guess we thought I could get in trouble or something, like Procter & Gamble would sue me or some such ridiculous thing. But that lasted about ten minutes. We came to our senses and realized what a goldmine we had, and I called the Mitchell brothers right away and told them. They were pretty excited too, and we met and talked about how they were going to release the news to the public and make use of it, and when they finally did, I was disappointed. They just kind of let it slip out rather than making a big thing out of it. It's become a big thing; it's worked for a long time and still fascinates people. It's the kinkiest, almost near-unbelievable gimmick ever, one that never could have been planned.

PORNO STAR ON IVORY SNOW BOX!

99 & 44/100% PURE COVER GIRL SUCKS COCK ON SCREEN!

PROCTER & GAMBLE UNKNOWINGLY HELPS PROMOTE PORNOGRAPHY!

IVORY SNOW AIN'T SO PURE ANYMORE!

There were all kinds of headlines in all kinds of papers. It was an interesting phenomenon (and still is, but Procter & Gamble is now in the process of replacing my face with a drawing, and I doubt if it'll look like me!) and people flocked to the theaters to see this person with two personalities, but they found out that the personality on the box was the same as the one in the movie, and that's my appeal and always will be. The image I project is one of being wholesome, clean, and all-American. That's why Procter & Gamble chose me. As I said, difficult to live up to, but very effective for selling soap.

About the soap—let's clean this up once and for all. The executives at Procter & Gamble must have gone a little crazy when they started reading that their current cover girl was the star of pornographic movies (*Eve* was released just at the time the Ivory Snow thing was at its height, and the picture benefited greatly because of it.) The first announcement they (Procter & Gamble) made was, "We have no knowledge of Miss Chambers' activities since 1970, when she posed for the photograph." The spokesman for the company would answer no questions and refused any further comment. Finally, bugged by reporters and interviewers for a long time, they made the announcement, "The current box is just not consistent with the image we are trying to portray," and they announced to the world that a new box was on its way. I wonder if sales went down because uptight housewives turned to Tide, but I doubt it—I think the controversy helped both of us.

You want to know something silly? I do use Ivory Snow when I do my wash. It's the least I can do after what they did for me!

Well, *Green Door* and Ivory Snow were part of my life, and it was inevitable that I do another film for the Mitchells. I knew *Eve* would be my last porno film for a while. You can't just keep going on that same level, you either go up or down, you have to take that chance. If you don't have the talent, you flop, but at least you tried. I hate people who always play it safe. And there I was in Walnut Creek, wondering who was going to help me make the transition to other things besides porno movies. It was a rough time for me because deep down inside I felt that Doug wasn't going to be part of my future. Ambition had no place in his life, yet it was a definite part of mine. I could see that something would happen, that the end would come, but I didn't want to face it and thus I just sat around for a long time, wondering what I was going to do. I was getting good money from the films and I knew I had enough financial security to take a stab at something else, at singing or dancing or a movie or the theater. The only time I envied Linda Lovelace was when I read that she was going to do a Vegas act. "That should be me!" I screamed. But I didn't know how to go about jumping off the plateau of "porno star" to some other kind of star. So I sat and brooded.

I also masturbated a lot.

And while I sat in my little house with a white picket fence, thousands of people were watching me fuck my brains out in *The Resurrection of Eve*....

6

The Resurrection of Eve

We knew *Eve* was going to be a smash when we made it. It was going to ride the crest of the *Green Door*/Ivory Snow wave, and we knew that people would come see it no matter what was in it. But the Mitchells wanted to make a good film and so did I. I got to talk in this one. Again, I'm too close to it to say how good it is (Chuck says it's not one of his favorites), but I know it was something else to film, and it has been very successful.

Porno films turn me on, and *Eve* definitely gives me a tingle in my pussy. I like a lot of the sex in that movie, and I think some of the love scenes are exciting and beautiful. When I made *Green Door* I really got off on the fantasy part of it, that wonderfully degrading, enjoyable fantasy that's as male chauvinist piglike as anything can be. The Women's League For Some Such Shit will kill me for that, but it's true.

I'm not into feminism. I'm into being feminine. That's what I am in *Eve*, and that's what I got off on in the making of the picture—the fact that it is really geared toward the woman's point of view. The guy presses her into swinging, which she rejects, but finally accepts it and digs it. *He* doesn't like it, then, because she comes off the winner in the end. I've talked to a lot of men who didn't like the film because of that; their egos felt threatened. Men's egos, my God! They're so crazy, so fucked up! Why do they feel so threatened all the time? I really don't understand it. *Eve* shows that women have sexual feelings too, they're not plastic. Women have sexual fantasies that turn them on. I like dominant men, strong men, but not those who are strong simply because they feel a woman threatening them. I like men who are strong because they are men, period.

The storyline of *Eve* is as complicated as *Green Door* is simple, and it seems less confusing when you read what the story is about than when you see it. The part of *Eve* is played by two women. I'm one of them. The "new" Eve. (A girl named Mimi Morgan plays the first one).

Here's what happens: Eve falls madly in love with Frank Paradise (Matthew Armand). Frank likes her, he thinks she's all right, but he's into a lot of chicks and she doesn't particularly satisfy him. Eve has a close friend, a black prizefighter (Johnnie Keyes again), and Frank starts to get these paranoid vibes that Eve and Johnnie are fucking. There's a scene I like where Frank and Eve are fucking in bed and he keeps flashing on Eve being in bed with the black prizefighter, and he lets his head get all fucked around because of it, and Eve wants to ball but he loses his hard-on, and so on. Anyway, Frank feels his masculinity threatened and he and Eve have a big fight, a really violent argument, which Frank has started, asshole that he is, and Eve freaks out because Frank is shouting at her about her balling a black guy and thinking she's gonna have spade kids or something, which is ridiculous anyway because Eve never made it with Johnnie.

So. Eve runs out of the house and jumps into the car and the tears steam down her face as she's driving, hysterical, and *bang!* She's in an accident that tears up her face and mutilates her beyond recognition. Time for cosmetic surgery, as they now call it! (I think it's a riot that Eve not only gets a new face, but an entire new body—mine. I think I should have played the early Eve in dumpy makeup or something, because you can't help but laugh when they unveil the new "face" and there's a whole new set of boobs and cunt and legs and arms to go with it.)

Eve goes to the hospital where she gets her new face. The bandages come off and Eve is now beautiful (enter *me*, you see). Frank rushes to the hospital and he's zonked out by the new Eve. He swears undying love and fidelity forever and he sweeps her from the hospital, marries her, and they live a life of connubial bliss. Frank does his thing—working as a disc jockey at a local radio station—and Eve does hers— vacuuming the carpet—and they're happy and fucking up a storm.

But everything is not well. No, the vacuum cleaner works fine, Eve is happy. It's Frank who has the problem. He's still getting hot over other chicks, making passes, getting uptight when Eve wants to suck his cock. He tries to put the make on a girl and she really puts him down: "Sorry, Frank, but I don't date married men."

So Frank gets the bright (and extremely male) idea that the answer to the problem is to get Eve to loosen up, via some swinger parties around town. Eve is fine. I mean she's happy with her dirty rug and vacuum cleaner and Frank's cock. What does she need swinger parties for? A Tupperware party, maybe, but a sex party? Forget it.

But she goes, reluctantly, because she loves Frank and he says she must try it.

Party time! The first one is a bacchanal, all kinds of people walking around in Greek togas and Roman gowns, a tit hanging our here, a cock there. Eve spends the evening dabbing her eyes in the powder room, where she sits on the toilet seat in anguish, hearing the squishing sounds of love being made in the other room, love being made by Frank, among others.

And there are more. Frank drags her around the circuit, from a '50s rock'n'roll ball to a *The Damned* costumed decadence gathering. After the first party Frank tells Eve that she's a "stone cold fox" for not getting into sucking or fucking anyone. True, Eve remained the essence of virginity at the first soiree. But she promises to do better at the second, to make Frank proud of her. So she fucks somebody at the second party, at Frank's request, but she hates it. Or does she? We find out at the third, the '50s party, where she seems to be starting to dig getting it on with someone other than good ol' Frank. At the next one she's a hit, everyone's trying to ball her, and by the fifth party, she's the *star!*

That fifth party is liberation day for our Eve.

And paranoia time for our Frank. Frank Paradise has swung out. He's jealous. His chick is digging other men. That's not right! He wants Eve all to himself. It's rough on Frank because Eve has not only discovered the wonders of sex and her (new) body, but a new self, a liberated self-liberated of her need for Frank. Frank wants it to go back to the way it was, the good ol' days when Eve vacuumed that floor with such passion and sucked only on his cock, no one else's.

Eve can't go back. She wants to explore the way it is, not the way it was.

Frank is one fucked-up guy as Eve announces, "It's over, Frank."

I realize it's not quite "Frankly, my dear, I don't give a damn," but then it's not trying to be.

One review said:

"Resurrection of Eve is undoubtedly one of the best pornographic films ever made. Technically, it signals the end of jumpy cinematography and inconsistent soundtrack. In fact, many of its scenes compare with the best that Hollywood can shoot. The storyline is believable and interesting. The actors and actresses are both physically attractive and competent—a sharp contrast to the pallid, unattractive, and mute players in previous pornographic movies."

My personal feeling is that the Mitchell brothers tried to cram too much into one film. However, I've got a lot of groovy memories about making it:

I thought the guy who played Frank—Armand—was sexy. I really enjoyed doing the film with him, I mean, acting in the clothed scenes as well as the fucking scenes. I suck his cock a lot in the film, and I really loved doing it. I guess I'm saying I liked his cock. Yeah, that's what I'm saying. I liked sucking his cock a lot. It sounds silly but I even remember when he came it tasted really sweet. I'd almost start to giggle, thinking, If only they knew how much I'm enjoying this!

I thought he was pretty good as Frank. A friend of mine pointed out that whenever he got mad or had a heavy scene to play he'd "start doing Hamlet." I cracked up—I don't know how my friend noticed it, but he did—because Armand was a Shakespearean actor, and was in fact appearing in a production of *Hamlet* when we shot *Eve*. Now when I see the film again I hear a little of Macbeth in Frank's speech pattern and see a little King Lear in his walk. It cracks me up.

Armand is a good actor and I think he felt really uptight all the time we filmed the movie. It was his first porno film and I'm sure his last. Why? Well, I think the male ego really goes through the wringer making a film like *Eve*. You're expected to be the stud, to have a hard cock waving in the air all the time, and that's a hard image to live up to and it puts you under a lot of pressure. And, too, for a serious actor to do a porno film, well, to him that isn't serious acting, and I used to tell Armand, "Look, it's cool, don't worry!" But it was rough on him. We worked very well together because I had done *Green Door*. I knew what was happening and he was very receptive to my suggestions, which were made mostly to put him at ease. Put him at ease and make his cock stay hard. That's the way I liked it best.

I really like the scene where Eve gives him a blowjob and his cock goes to black, where he's imagining me in bed with Johnnie Keyes. I thought that was a gas to do, because I had to shoot the scene with both guys, and I think it comes off well on screen. And it's a trip, seeing a guy's big white dick change to a big black dick and then back and all the time the chick stays the same. It's erotic, and yet it's effective in another sense, in that you say to yourself, "Poor Frank, he's really getting fucked up!" I thought Armand was really good in that scene, and I mean all of him, not only his cock.

Anyway, he went back to Shakespeare.

You know, it's almost campy at times when Frank starts enunciating as though we're doing one of the classics. I think the Mitchell brothers knew that and considered it an "in" joke. They filled that film with all kinds of private jokes. Some people don't dig that kind of thing. Some don't want humor in a sex film, and especially not that kind of humor. It isn't slapstick or broad comedy, it's a kind of "guffaw behind the scenes" and only certain people pick up on it. But the Mitchells made the film and they could do what they wanted.

I think they write mainly for their own fantasies, what turns them on, what happened to a friend of theirs, drawing things only from their little family, the "in" jokes that the audience really doesn't understand or care about. They're the opposite of someone like Gerry Damiano, whose movies are really very serious and require some heavy thinking on the part of the audience. I think both have their extremes though and I prefer something in the middle, like *Green Door*.

People go to sex films to be relieved of life, to get rid of their heavy problems and enjoy themselves and get turned on. If they come to a film all about sex, but also all about suicide or something like that, they're not going to come out whistling. Again, if the whole thing's too ridiculous and funny they won't have experienced a sexual thrill and they'll feel cheated. I think sex films should give the audience a hard-on.

And I think people shouldn't have to think a lot when seeing a sex film. They shouldn't have to figure things out. There are movies for that, brilliant movies like *Chinatown*. Sex films should be viewed with your hands between your legs. You should be able to play with yourself and enjoy it and not have to sit and consciously think what it's all about. The plot should be simple enough for that. And if there's a lot of fucking and sucking in a film, there isn't room for a lot of plot. Again, leave that up to other films. It it's a sex film, that's what it's all about. It's jerk-off time, not thinking time.

So let's not think. Let's jerk off. I think the most fun in filming *Eve* was the '50s party, the rock'n'roll scene. I loved it 'cause I got to dance, first of all, and it was a step back in time. I had been too young to go to dances like that in the real '50s. But I remember them happening. And the sex part of it is a real fantasy trip because not many people were balling back in the '50s, so I'm told. In those first few party scenes, I had to restrain myself from showing that I liked it—I was supposed to be Eve and she was uptight and not ready to accept having sex with any man but Frank. I thought of all of it as work, of course, but to see all those naked people around you, all those cocks being gobbled by lips and cunts, it can get you horny. Hell, it nearly drove me nuts, but I didn't tell anyone. I played it cool. I probably went into the ladies' room and masturbated or something!

The toga party was rough for me to do. I sat in a goddamned bathroom while everyone fucked! There I sat, contemplating the toilet paper, while everybody was taking their clothes off and getting their rocks off. An interesting thing in doing that scene (and all the party scenes) was getting that many people together at one time and then getting them all to have sex at one time. You probably noticed that the group of people is rather bizarre, and they wanted them to be weird, strange, kinky. There's the black chick in the party scenes and she always has a prick in her mouth. You never see her without a dick to suck on. You watch the film and say, "Oh, my God, there she is again, going down on another one!" Maybe she was born with a cock in her mouth and that's why the Mitchells chose her. She sure enjoyed sucking, that's for sure. Someone would yell, *"Cut!"* and she would go right on until you'd have to pull her off the guy's dick.

Everyone's there at the same time for those party scenes, but the sex scenes, the individual close-ups, are done separately, or as separately as possible. It isn't one big massive orgy or anything (which I think is less exciting than having the actors and crew all sitting around watching everyone take their turns at balling on camera). If a wide-angle shot is done, then everyone must be doing it, everyone must be getting it on or at least look as though they are. But the real fun comes in the smaller shots, where a couple, or three people, or any number (depending on the sex in the scene) of people, can really make it in front of the camera. There's a kind of excitement in knowing that while you're sucking off some guy the camera is taking a close-up of you. It makes it more fun than a big group scene where you don't know if you're in the shot at all or if the camera is catching what you're doing. But when you have that lens and all those people staring at you, you know that blowjob you're giving is going to show up on the screen in all its vivid glory. So it had better be good!

I think the filming of *Eve* took two months, a lot longer than *Green Door* had taken. There were so many details to film, and also, because of the rather involved plot, the film couldn't be shot in any kind of sequence. That's another reason why I think simplicity of plot is better. Another thing about the orgy scenes—if the director stood there and said, "Go!" and all the action started and it was up to the camera to try and get everyone, long shots as well as close-ups, you'd probably have everyone coming at the same time. Orgasms turn people on, they're the ultimate moments in sex films, just as they're the ultimate moment is sex. People want to see guys shooting their jism on the screen. If you shot an orgy straight—meaning if everyone just started balling at the same time—they'd probably reach climaxes at the same time, and the camera would be able to catch only one of those in a close shot. So it's better to do them separately.

One of my favorite scenes is a typical one from real life. Frank and I are fucking and in the middle of it, he starts to talk to me about swinging. We're carrying on, his cock is sliding in and out of me and I'm lost in pleasure, and all of a sudden, he says, "Well, did you think about it yet?" And I say, "What?" And he goes on rapping about this thing he wants her to do. Well, the way to get a woman to do something is not to stop in the middle of a wonderful fuck and start rapping with her! I think a lot of people identify with that scene. They laugh at it when it happens on screen because it is funny, but later I think they realize that the reason they were laughing is that the same thing happens to them. I mean, Frank wants an answer from Eve right then and there, with his dick sill inside her. It's as if he has her pinned to the bed and she has to agree with whatever he says. And that's when Eve gets herself committed to swinging, and Frank follows up on it, of course. That moment of passion is not the time to get a woman's true feelings on any subject.

Getting back to the different people involved in the film, the crazy assortment of humanity the Mitchells picked both for the "audience" in *Green Door* and the swingers in *Eve*. There is a huge chick in *Green Door*, an enormous girl, and a little skinny guy who stands on a chair and dives into her cunt as though he were jumping off the high board. They're married. Yup. Married. And they seem very *happily* married. I think it's probably a mother complex with the guy, but if that works out, fine. "Smother me, mother!" What's wild about them is that they can't keep their hands off each other; they're the most oversexed people I've ever known. It's incredible because they were always feeling each other and kissing, and, whenever they had the chance during the filming, fucking.

One day the big chick was down on a couch. The guy, the skinny little husband, was between her legs, feeling her and fondling her pussy and turning her on. Finally, she gasped and bent over to kiss him and she pushed forward so hard that the whole couch gave up and died. *Crash.* The legs broke and it fell to the floor and she looked up with an expression like "what hit me?" And everyone was laughing and she realized what had happened and started apologizing for it and all through it, her little husband was eating her pussy. It didn't even bother him. And this whole scene wasn't even on camera—this was on a break! We all acted like it was nothing, and we laughed, but we all thought, these two characters are something else!

Another scene that was a trip for me, even though I wasn't involved in it, was the opening scene in the film, the fantasy thing when Eve is supposed to be young. See, I always get off on fantasies. Anyway, I say, "supposed to be young" because the chick playing it was anything but young. That's the scene where the Merchant Marine teaches young Eve about sex, making love first to her doll and then to her, finally getting her to suck his cock just as her mother enters and goes nuts. The guy playing the part is Dale Meader, who's also in *Green Door*. He's a good actor and he can be very obscene-looking. It's quite a fantasy, the old man teaching a young virgin about sex.

But the girl should have looked fourteen. She was, in reality, twenty, but it was still ludicrous. All that makeup and stuff they put on her. She says, "I'm twelve," and you say, "What's this baloney." Thirty would be a better guess. I watched that scene being shot and you could almost see the perspiration dripping off Dale's cock. Hot. One thing the

Mitchell brothers don't know too much about is lights. We used to think they were out to fry us. I thought the heat was going to singe the hair on my pussy!

I think the "idea" of that scene is what I really turn on to, the thing of having an older man, a sailor yet, telling me what it's like to feel sexual pleasure for the first time, and then eating my pussy after he eats my doll's snatch, and then teaching me how to suck his big cock. I had that fantasy when I was young and I think most girls have it. The girl's mother comes in and sees her twelve-year-old daughter giving head to the guy she picked up and freaks out! That's part of the fantasy too, always worrying that your mother will catch you—every girl has that when she masturbates. I think it provides even more stimulation—that chance of getting caught doing something that is "naughty."

You know, no one ever got a disease filming those two pictures. When you cast for extras in a fuck film, you never know what you're going to get—especially when your extras are as bizarre as the Mitchell brothers' extras. I demanded that everyone in *Green Door* and *Eve* have a VD test before we started shooting, mainly because I knew that on an earlier film one chick had given the clap to the entire cast! And she knew it. She hadn't gotten a starring role and out of spite, she gave VD to every damn person in the film. The Mitchells wondered why she was suddenly so damned sex crazy, like she kept going from one cock to another, one pussy to another, in the orgy scenes, carrying on like crazy, passing her little secret around to everyone. The Mitchells found out soon enough. So it's never happened again.

People call up and write and say, "I'll be in your next film." You have to be careful there. As Chuck says, "That person could turn out to be a cop. *Deep Throat II* had a cop on the set and we just played games with him till he left, 'cause we'd been tipped off and knew who he was. It's great to be busted after the film has opened, because it means free publicity and a line of people at the box office. But it just costs money and time if it happens while you're shooting.

The extras used in legit films in Hollywood belong to an extras' union, which is a very tight clique. Same thing with fuck film extras, though they're not in a union. They're a tight clique. That's why you'll see many of the same people in all the Mitchell brothers' films. Directors know their extras and they like to use people who they know will work out. They don't want a guy who will suddenly turn into superstud in the middle of an orgy scene and walk up and wave his hard dick into the camera. They want him to do what he's being paid to do. They don't want a chick who will suddenly freeze up and lock her pussy tight when the camera is trying to catch the guy starting to ball her. They want her to be natural, as though she doesn't know the camera is there. In the early days of fuck films, they used to just pick up freaks from the streets of Haight Ashbury and pay them a few bucks to fuck on screen. Today it isn't that way; most of the extras are known to the Mitchells and they just call them up and tell them when the next film is shooting.

In fact, the fuck film extras have formed a "kind" of union, meaning that they have a spokesman for the group and have demanded a certain pay scale. Even the Screen Actors' Guild recently started sending people to an X-film casting call here in New York. The Mitchell brothers weren't very happy when the group started demanding what they felt was decent pay, but they had no choice. Fuck films had surfaced.

The Mitchell brothers, Jim and Artie, had started out doing small, junky, 8mm fuck films (loops) just like everyone else. They're both average, down-home kind of guys. Some people would call them hicks because they're not sophisticated, and I think most people think of filmmakers as being very intelligent and sophisticated. They're both married. Art has four children and loves them to death and they have a beautiful house. Jim is married to a wonderful chick. They both lead separate lives apart from their work, but they share the same sense of humor and that's what makes them so likeable.

We were friends and business partners, which was a good marriage until Chuck took over the business aspect of my career. Then the friendship ended. I really don't know why it had to, but it did. They told Chuck I was nothing, that I had sucked some spades on screen and that was as much as I was ever going to do, that I was washed up. I felt hurt because these guys were supposed to be my managers; they were supposed to promote my career! Filmmakers they are, managers they're not. Chuck got me out of my contract with them because the same lawyer (theirs) had drawn up my papers without my even getting a look at them, and it isn't considered fair or ethical for the same attorney to represent people on opposite sides of the same fence. So their "agreement" was null and void because of the legal loopholes in its construction. Chuck says, "When I first met the Mitchells, I was totally unimpressed. I knew some of the biggest people in the business and I figured these guys were just a couple of fucking rednecks. I thought they were stupid, because they had a film that's probably made twelve million when it could have made twenty-four million. They're penny-wise and dollar-foolish. Instead of mass distribution, they handle it themselves. *Deep Throat* was mass distributed, which means it lost ten percent right off the top, but who cares—the people who owned it made twenty-something million dollars off it. You can afford to lose ten percent of that.

"The Mitchells rent a theater someplace in some town and they put their own movies into it and thus make sure no one gets a dollar off them. Instead of playing in ten theaters, they'll play in one. And they were foolish about Marilyn—publicity means bread. They said, 'Who cares about her, so she sucked off a few guys on film, big deal.' "That's when it was time for me to take over."

The Mitchells made their first erotic film, *Daydreams*, in Art's flat in Haight Ashbury. By 1969, they'd made enough bread to buy their own theater and production company—The Mitchell Brothers Film Group. They sent out a release, which said, "The Film Group is a unique company that operates more as a family than a typical bureaucratic business. For example, when a film is being made, everyone from the cashiers to office personnel becomes involved." Okay.

The O'Farrell Theater, which was once a restaurant until Art and Jim renovated it to become the headquarters for the film group and the primary showplace for all Mitchell films, is a large corner building painted bright colors. It's on the corner of Polk and O'Farrell streets, and it's almost a landmark in San Francisco. Whatever the Mitchells' faults, they sure have been a prime force in the changing face of pornography in this country. And they gave me my big break. I think the ultimate way to watch a porno film—and someone should build a theater like this—is to be able to lie back on a mattress or something and watch it on the ceiling. That way you can take off your clothes and play with yourself, use a vibrator, do anything you want with yourself or with others, and really feel the stimulation of the flick. You can even fuck like crazy while watching a fuck film. It's terrific. Wouldn't it be great to watch that final come scene in *Green Door* and have a guy doing that to you at the same moment? What an ultimate fantasy trip! You could be watching the cream shoot all over the face on screen while hot sticky cum is actually shooting onto your face at the same moment! It would be wild for the guy too; he would be seeing on screen what is happening down between his legs! Wow, what a trippy thought!

What's an erotic film really supposed to do? Turn people on, first of all. I really believe that. I have a friend who writes fuck books. The first thing he keeps in mind is the fact that someone's going to jerk off while reading it. That's why they buy it, and he has to give them the chance to get hard and get their rocks off. Same thing with porno films—they have to be able to give people a sense of sexual stimulation. I think they owe that to the audience. Just as a musical is meant to entertain, as its prime purpose, a fuck film is meant to excite.

But they can do many other things too. Many of the current chic porno films don't turn people on physically, they turn them on mentally. It may become physical later, when they get home, but in the theater, it's a mental trip, learning something new about sex, feeling free and loose, getting ready to try what is up on the screen. You'll always have the guys coming in with the raincoats, but not all films are geared for that. The loops are still around, if that's what you want—just hard-core jack-off material.

Porno films also entertain and amuse and teach. That stimulation is there—it has to be—that stimulation of your fantasies—not necessarily your physical self, though that may be part of it, but your sexual fantasies. Big porno films induce your fantasies. They're a jumping-off point for your own sex trip. Loops are nothing, but fast masturbation films.

And porno audiences are now of a higher caliber, better educated, brighter, not quite so uptight as the last generation. The nice-looking young couple from the suburbs have replaced the dirty old man with no teeth, a three-day-old beard, and one hand frozen in a cock-whacking position.

A friend of mine recently told me a far-out story. His very together seventeen-year-old brother and his twenty-five-year-old brother and his father all went to see *Green Door* and *Eve*. What a trip, especially for their dad! At first, they said they were a little shocked. I could imagine their father thinking, God, what am I doing here with my boys? But then they got used to it and they all started digging it, each in his own way. My friend told me that his dad went home and got it on with his wife like never before, he was so horny to try a few new things, a few positions they hadn't tried in years. The twenty-five-year-old brother said he beat off like crazy that night, like there was no stopping. And the seventeen-year-old—he's just getting into a sex trip with his girlfriend—said they had the best time the following evening in his car. I just hope it wasn't raining.

Three guys, seventeen, twenty-five, and fifty, all seeing a porno double bill, then going to have a pizza afterward and admitting it was a turn-on, but not a physical turn-on in the theater, that it had stimulated imaginations and fantasies somewhere inside of them. And then it became physical later, in their own private moments. And I think that's great.

I love the fact that sex films teach. Lots of girls don't know how to put a guy's dick in their mouth, they don't know how to really move their tongue over the head and lick down the shaft and do the little lip movements that drive men bananas. Seeing that up on the screen can really tell them something about technique. In the off-Broadway musical *Let My People Come* there's a skit entitled "Fellatio 101" ... a bunch of girls, sitting in class, are taught the fine art of cocksucking by a horny old bag of a schoolmarm, and they practice on bananas. It's a riot, but it also points up what I'm saying—that people need to be taught sex technique. What better place to learn it than a porno theater? Better than a sterile classroom. Why not be entertained and educated at the same time?

I learned a lot in *making* the films. It was good practice, having all those different cocks to play with, all those different balls to hold in my hands and caress. I would notice the reaction of each individual guy, and I soon learned what turned them on the most, what was the best way to nibble at their pricks or fondle them or tickle them with my tongue. It was great fun and so exciting—and I'd go home and tell Doug that I'd had a ball filming that day and he'd say, "Well, show me what you did," and I'd just pull down his jeans as he flopped on the bed and start recreating exactly what I'd done at work. When I'm doing my nightclub act now, I get fantasies of sucking off all the guys in the audience. I really think about that, and it helps me come across to them, it makes me reach out to them. I communicate better with the audience that way. Sex is a great way to communicate. Great!

So I made *Eve,* and Doug and I communicated sexually and we had a great life, or so I wanted to believe. But I was getting restless, bored. Nothing was happening in my life. Finally, the Mitchell brothers asked if I wanted to go to Europe for the opening of *Green Door*, and I said sure, anything to be doing something! And after Europe, I was going to open *Eve* at the World Theater in New York, and it was while I was in New York that Linda Lovelace walked out on Chuck Traynor in Los Angeles.

Marilyn standing front & center with her Mom, sister Jan and brother Bill Briggs, in front of their home in Westport CT.

Marilyn on her wedding day to Douglas Chaplin at Mt. Tamalpais Park in Mill Valley California. 1972.

Courtesy of Mark Cox.

MARILYN CHAMBERS is "Angel of H.E.A.T."

MARILYN CHAMBERS

Courtesy of Mark Cox.

On the set of *Insatiable* with Richard Pachecho. Howie Gordon Archives.

Marilyn with make up
artist David Clark.
Howie Gordon Archives.

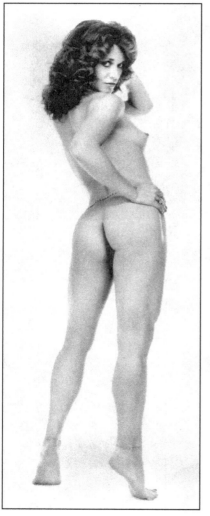

Taken at Marilyn's Las Vegas home in September 1976.
From the collection of Mark Cox.

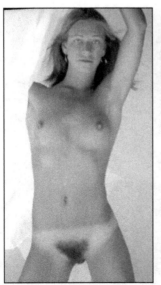

On Thursday, December 3, 1998, crowds withstood the California rain for as much as six hours to get into the grand opening of the world's premier erotic boutique, HUSTLER HOLLYWOOD.

The Porn Walk of Fame has arrived! The first three inductees—legends Larry Flynt, Ron Jeremy and Marilyn Chambers—impress their famous flesh for posterity.

On your way to the fully stocked coffee and juice bar, take macho harlot Janine's advice, and pick up a few leather novelties—or else.

Marilyn Chambers when she was inducted in the HUSTLER HOLLYWOOD Walk of Fame.

Courtesy of Mark Cox.

Taken at Marilyn's Las Vegas home in March 1979. From the
collection of Mark Cox.

At a Las Vegas raquet club in October 1978. From the
collection of Mark Cox.

Taken at Marilyn's Las Vegas
home in 1977. From the
collection of Mark Cox.

Taken April 1975 in the Las Vegas desert. From the
collection of Mark Cox.

Taken at Marilyn's Hollywood home in June 1976. From the
collection of Mark Cox.

Courtesy of Mark Cox.

Marilyn with Charles Jay years after running for Vice President with Jay
for President in 2004's Personal Choice Party.

7

The Resurrection of Marilyn

I had wanted to meet Linda Lovelace for a long time. I wanted to know what she was like, where her head was at—after all, she was my only real competition and she seemed to have it made. I envied her position. I'm still asked what she's like, on almost every interview, and the fact is that I never met her and now I don't ever care to. I guess people think that all porno stars know each other, that Linda, Georgina, Tina, and Marilyn get together every Wednesday afternoon and gossip and knit or something. We'd probably sit around making French ticklers if that happened. Some sorority, huh?

The fact is, we don't know each other, not all of us, and there is nothing binding us together other than the fact that we're in the same business. But I wanted to make a connection with Linda and I had tried—once. I called, trying to get through to Linda, just to say "hi" or something, and I got Chuck Traynor instead. I'd forgotten all about this until recently. I guess I must have sounded like a real jerk because we didn't talk more than a minute—Chuck cut me off, he wouldn't let me talk with Linda. He was very protective of her; she was his wife.

And I was just another name on the screen.

We almost connected one other time. I knew a girl, Carol, and she had shot a nude male calendar, the Ladies Home Companion Calendar, and Doug had been in it. Yes, Doug, my Doug. If his wife could do fuck films, why couldn't he show his body in a photo? I had done something for *Playboy* and the photographer's friend was Carol's husband and he's the guy who did The Tit.

The Tit is a mold of my boob, the left one (my first lover would freak out, he never touched the left one!), in a clear plastic block. It's very hard to describe, you have to see it. It looks like crystal, solid, and you have to look at it in the light to see what's in it. It's my boob with fingers around it. I think it's a gas. But you have to see it. I know it sounds dumb.

Anyhow, that's how we got to know Carol, Douglas and I, and when she was doing the shooting of Doug, I asked her if she had ever met Linda Lovelace. She said sure, she knew her and liked her, but she liked her husband, Chuck Traynor, even better, that he was a terrific guy. "I'll have him call you if you want to meet Linda so bad," she said.

So that's what made Chuck call the Mitchell brothers, not me. He knew they were my managers and he didn't want to talk to me, he wanted to talk business. He was dreaming up a film starring Linda Lovelace and Marilyn Chambers. Well, he couldn't get through to the Mitchell brothers so he did call me finally. The second time I'd ever talked with him. He told me he wanted to do a film starring Linda and me. I should have jumped for joy and said, "Terrific, when do we start?" But instead I got cold and said, "Speak to my managers, I'm too busy," and hung up. Can you believe that? At that time he was at a high peak with Linda, his notoriety was hitting the sky and he was very powerful, and who the hell was I to say, "Speak to my managers." Jesus, my managers didn't even give a damn about my career at that point.

I asked Chuck what he thought of me when I hung up on him, and he said, "I thought you were the stupidest broad on earth. Linda was dumb, I knew that, but you took first place." Chuck figured he'd be doing me a big favor by putting me in a film with Linda, but when I gave him that line on the phone he figured fuck it, forget it, he didn't need me.

And at that time, he didn't know the situation I was in, that the Mitchells weren't really doing anything for me and I was worried about the future. He had been watching me and my career very closely because he believed strongly that only one superstar would rise out of the "porno cult of the '70s" and he of course wanted it to be Linda. I was the only competition around, but after that phone call, he was pretty sure I could never give Linda a run for her money. I was no big threat 'cause I was dumb.

Well, he was right, at the time. I was dumb to be letting the Mitchells handle my career. I needed someone like Chuck but I didn't know where to find him. You see, everything about Linda Lovelace had been planned; nothing happened by accident. The gimmick of "deep throat," the film's promotion, the association with Sammy Davis and Hefner, the appearances at all the chic parties in Beverly Hills—everything was carefully manufactured by Chuck Traynor. Linda was no accident.

I was. I answered an ad by accident and got *Green Door*. Ivory Snow turns up on the supermarket shelves the week *Green Door* opens. Then *Eve* takes off. Pure accident. Promotion and management is everything, meaning that planning is everything. It has to be pursued twenty-four hours a day. With the Mitchells, I was Marilyn Chambers (a name they gave me because it sounded very plain and nice and WASPish) on screen and a few hours a week at openings or interviews, but the rest of the time I was Marilyn Briggs, housewife. Now, with Chuck, I'm Marilyn Chambers every minute of the day and night.

For example, Chuck won't let me go to an opening in jeans, on a bicycle. I go in a limousine, wearing a white ermine coat. I think the public wants the image of a superstar to remain part of life; they don't want to see the old Hollywood die. Stars aren't glamorous anymore, and I think they should be. We grew up loving the image of Elizabeth Taylor in gowns and jewels riding in a white Rolls. I don't want to see that end. It's a great fantasy, it's relief from the lousy situation of the world today.

Elizabeth Taylor. Fantasies. That brings back another fantasy I had when I was younger. I used to masturbate thinking of this all the time, especially on lonely days in New York when I had nothing to do and the phone didn't ring and the sky was dark and I felt down. I would dream of myself being a great Hollywood star, driving up to a beautiful Gatsby-like mansion in a white Rolls-Royce, dressed in white mink.

I would get out of the car and the doorman would greet me and just as I would be walking to the front door, it opened and out walked the most beautiful man in the world, the man of the house, dressed in formal attire, looking radiant and elegant and handsome….

We are introduced and he asks me to go for a walk around the grounds, before going into the party, which he calls "rather boring." So I take his arm and we walk among the trees and fountains of the beautiful estate and finally end up near a large pond filled with goldfish, sitting on a wicker loveseat with a bottle of champagne next to us, on ice. He would tell me how much he loved my movies and how grateful he was that I had come to his party. Then he kisses my hand and presses it between his legs, where I feel a huge bulge, already hard in his undershorts under the silken material of his formal striped trousers.

I look into his eyes and they are endless and I still feel his cock growing under my palm, getting warmer and warmer, and I can even feel the hard ridge around the tip as we begin to run our tongues inside each other's mouths.

Then he says, "Blow me." Just like that, arrogant and richlike, stuffy, but he is so beautiful I'll do anything for him....

I fall to my knees in my white gown and let the mink slip down to the ground. I open the buttons on his crotch with my teeth and lick his cock through his silk underpants. Then I carefully unlatch the waistband and the tip of his huge organ springs up and stares me in the face. It is wet already in my mouth, pulling his shorts down under his balls so I can take the entire length of his dick, all nine inches, into my throat, sucking on it like crazy. I have an orgasm as I'm giving him deep throat and he sighs and cries out and then pulls his dick from my mouth just as he is ready to come. He bucks his ass into the air and a fountain of jism squirts from his dickhead and splashes all over my face, my furs, my satin gown ... all over his black silken jacket and his impeccably white shirt. He groans and I lick the jism from my cheek and from the pulsating tip of his cock....

"Fuck me," I order, in the same tone he'd commanded me to blow him. I fall back on the ground and let him lift my skirt to my neck, exposing my naked breasts and wet, hairy cunt. He kneels above me, his tuxedo pants down around his ankles, over his patent leather shoes, and his cock is as hard as before he came and he shoves it into me after teasing my pussy lips with the big wet head. I scream in pleasure as I wrap my legs around his strong, hot, naked thighs, and I dig my fingers into his ass as his long cock digs into my pussy. We roll around on my mink, turning over and over, his cock slamming into me, until I gasp in pleasure and he muffles my scram with his lips as I reach a shattering orgasm.

Then he says, "I'm coming, I'm fucking coming again!" And he slams into me for one last time and I feel the hot wet jism filling my belly and I let him pump it into me, but as soon as he collapses on top of me I push him off and go down on him again, licking all the come and pussy juice from his beautiful softening cock.

Then, after we lie there looking up at the stars for a long time, never talking, he pours the bottle of champagne all over my body and licks it from me. He pours it into my pussy and then drinks it out. He lets it run down my ass and wet the mink and he rolls his head on my ass and licks the bubbly stuff off me. Then I pour some champagne on his cock and balls and lick them clean, and finally we stand up and he helps me back to my car and I drive off as he goes into his house to meet all the other famous people at his party....

In the car, on the way to my own mansion, I masturbate like crazy with the empty champagne bottle, reminding me of our wonderful scene and his memorable penis. I am not sure I will ever see him again. But it has been some of the greatest sex of my life....

Oh, the fantasies I had!

Anyhow, I was sitting around waiting for another accident to happen which would shoot me up above Linda Lovelace as a superstar. But one wasn't going to happen. Chuck says, "I'd kept a close eye on Marilyn even though I'd never met her. I knew she had a lot on the ball with the Ivory Snow thing, I knew *Green Door* was good, I knew she was younger than Linda. I didn't know if she could sing or dance, but I knew if Linda was going to get any heavy competition it would come from Marilyn. I had to plan ahead of the Mitchells. I overestimated them, I thought they were very together as managers, but they weren't. That phone call told me everything I wanted to know."

And dumb me, I put myself into the Mitchells' hands completely. After I hung up on Chuck that time, I thought, Big deal, big shit! Who does he think he is? All I'd wanted to do was meet Linda and sniff her out, see where her head was at. I didn't want to make a film with her. I had too much lousy pride.

So I was in New York for the opening of *Eve* at the World Theater and Chuck Traynor called me. But this time it was different, he was a different person. He had called and left a message for me to call back, that it was super important and urgent, to please call immediately, but I sat around for a while until he called me a second time.

Talking to him was amazing. It was like some kind of magic electricity was suddenly binding us.

There was electricity in that phone call, magic. I felt so strange—this wasn't the guy I'd talked to before. And I felt as though he were right there, not in Los Angeles. He told me Linda had taken a walk, which floored me. She had her Vegas act all put together and it was going to open in Miami for $25,000 a week. (That's when I had screamed in jealousy, when I'd read that just a few days before Chuck's phone call.) She was going to make a movie with Sammy Davis. All kinds of wonderful things. And she had just walked out on all of them. I couldn't believe it!

So supermanager, superhustler Chuck Traynor made a marvelous recovery when Linda announced she was leaving him behind (well, the truth is, on the inside, it hurt him a lot and it took a long time for him to get over her leaving). He asked me to take her place. This time I didn't tell him to call my managers. This time it wasn't an accident; this was planning. This time I swallowed my pride and said yes, immediately, without a moment's hesitation. It sounded too good to be true. Jump into Linda Lovelace's shoes? Would they fit? I didn't give a damn. I'd *make* them fit. I was sure I had more talent in my body than she had in her throat. I could and would take her place and do better than she would have down.

"How soon can you get here?" he asked.

"I don't know."

"The sooner the better."

"I'll call you back." I hung up and called Doug in San Francisco. (Just before I'd left for the opening of *Eve* in New York, for the Mitchell brothers' sponsored tour, Doug and I had moved back to the city from Walnut Creek. The days of suburban housewifery were over.) So I told Doug what Chuck had just offered me and he said it sounded like a good idea and that I should definitely go to Los Angeles and see what he had to offer. Doug never stood in my way; he knew a career was important to me. I think he was a bit jealous because I'd be away from him for a while, maybe even a long time, but he understood that I had something he didn't know how to deal with—ambition—and Chuck did know how to deal with such a drive.

I called Chuck back and said, "I'm on my way," and then caught the next plane for San Francisco, and there Doug helped me pack two suitcases and get on another plane for Los Angeles. It was a whirlwind. I knew I was going to be gone for a few months at least, however long it would take to get into the position Linda had been in. I had visions of opening in Vegas in two weeks, ridiculous things like that. My head was in the clouds. I was leaving my husband behind and going off to a guy I'd never even met.

Funny, but I really trusted Chuck, this guy I'd never met. I believed him. I knew it was going to happen. I was that sure of him, just from the sound of his voice. He was determined and he was strong.

It worked both ways. "I had no idea if she could sing, dance, or yodel, or anything," Chuck says, "but the sound of determination in her voice turned me on. I believed her when she said she could do those things. Well, maybe she can't yodel...."

Chuck has told me always to keep a question in mind: "Do you look into the future and hope for it, or do you make it happen?" He believes you make it happen. There is no future without working at it. He was determined to turn Marilyn Chambers into a superstar. He isn't the kind of guy who goes into an office asking himself, "Can I convince this guy...?" He walks in thinking, "I *know* I can convince him...."

I've always been superpositive in my thinking and I knew I needed something and someone to get me out of that *Green Door*-Ivory Snow-*Eve* rut. To get me off that plateau. I was beginning to realize that I wasn't going to get it from the Mitchells and I knew it wasn't going to come from Doug or, for that matter, anyone whom I'd been in contact with in the past. It had to be someone new, someone in the future. Here was the only opportunity I had and I had to take advantage of it. Chuck Traynor was waiting for me.

Leaving Douglas was strange. When I flew from New York to San Francisco, I started feeling jittery, as though my entire life were doing somersaults. When I got home to Doug, I got the most eerie feeling, as though everyone were dead. The morning I got up to leave for Los Angeles, I never felt worse in my life. As I said goodbye to Doug at the airport, I had the feeling that it was the last time I'd be saying goodbye to him as my husband. And I hadn't even really consciously thought of leaving him or breaking up with him. It had been a reality only deep in my soul and I never wanted to deal with it. It was very easy to be married to Douglas as long as I didn't have much of a career.

But when the plane took off and San Francisco was behind me, I had to deal with our marriage and what was happening. I still fought it, convincing myself that things would work out and maybe he'd move to Los Angeles and I'd be a big star but I'd still go home to him and let him cook the meals and we'd fuck like always and life would be terrific. But my life was changing. I was mixed up. I could see there really wasn't much of a marriage between us. I felt closer to a guy I'd only talked to on the phone than I felt to my own husband. That's a scary feeling. I guess Doug and I were two people clinging to each other because we didn't have anything else, wondering what would come next in our life of accidents and surprises. Well, I did have something else now, and the clinging had no reason for being anymore. The accidents and surprises were over. Except for one more surprise on Doug—the day I told him we were through. It really did surprise him.

I couldn't have gone on like that with Doug, wondering what was going to happen next in life. I wanted to *make* things happen; I was bored with waiting. That's why I fit so well into Chuck's life; I was into his attitude, into his thoughts about making the future work for you. Doug's attitude was no longer a part of me. I knew that, but still, on the plane I fought it and tried to tell myself I'd be back to San Francisco and everything would continue as before. Somehow.

But I was never to see our house in San Francisco again.

Well, I arrived in Los Angeles only to walk into one of the most embarrassing moments of my life. When I had last talked to Chuck before leaving San Francisco he'd told me either he'd be waiting for me or the limo driver would be there to meet me. Okay, swell. "The limo driver'll be in a black suit," he said. Great. So I get off the plane and I'm bouncing around and I see this guy in a black suit and a cap looking like he is supposed to meet someone, and I go up to him and say, "Hi! Here I am!" He nods and takes my bags and we start walking down the stairs and he says, "How was San Francisco, Mrs. Rubenstein?"

Mrs. who?

And at that moment, Chuck Traynor ran up and said, "Marilyn, you got the wrong guy!" God, it was embarrassing. The driver handed my bags back as Chuck handed me some flowers. There I was thinking the driver was waiting for me and I had wanted to make a good impression on Chuck, and I had almost been swept off to some unknown mansion owned by a Mrs. Rubenstein. I felt like a real fool. Oh, did I feel dumb.

So Chuck Traynor and I finally met. He didn't look at all as I'd pictured him. I was expecting a real freak with long hair, form some reason, and he turned out to be pretty straight-looking, and had a feeling of Los Angeles about him. I don't know how to really explain that, but there a type of "L. A. person" and Chuck felt like one. He is originally from Florida (his life story and how he met Linda and turned her into the star she was is amazing, and it's all in the next chapter) but he had assimilated into the L. A. scene very well by the time I'd met him.

And so we got into a limousine, went off to dinner, talked and talked and talked. For a week, day in and day out. I was being supercautious. For the contracts and all I had my lawyer fly down from San Francisco. I trusted Chuck but ever since the film *Together* I trusted lawyers more, my lawyers at least. I guess I put Chuck through all kinds of shit with the legal stuff, but he respected me for it because he could see that I was strong enough to care about what was happening to my future. And I liked him. He was the opposite of what I'd heard—that Chuck Traynor is a bastard and obnoxious and will ruin me. He was pleasant, intelligent, together. He rapidly became my best friend. I didn't feel I was clinging to him for survival, as I'd felt with Doug. I felt we were holding hands and walking on top of the world.

But there were no sexual goings-on at all. Nothing. That wasn't what we were there for. I had made it very clear, just as I'd made it clear to the Mitchell brothers, that I wanted a business relationship and not an emotional, physical one. I was still married, faithful to my husband. I didn't want an emotional mess to fuck up anything that could come from my business relationship. And Chuck agreed.

I never found out till very recently exactly what Chuck thought of me when we first met. I should preface it by quoting him on Hollywood and what stars are all about:

"Hollywood is attracted by the girl next door, as long as the girl next door has the right complexion, the right nails, the right jewelry, the right clothes. I had banged my head against the wall for two years trying to get Linda into that position, but she was just a kid, she didn't look right, she didn't walk right, she didn't do anything right. And she knew it. It was rough, Jesus, was it rough. We had the gimmick of 'deep throat' but we knew it wouldn't last forever. After the gimmick, you need something to sustain you in Hollywood, or you're finished. I wanted to turn Linda into a glamorous young star.

"And that's what I expected to see walk off that plane, Marilyn Chambers, glamorous young star. I expected her to look like what I'd pictured her to be in my head. I had seen those glossy stills from *Green Door*, the shots of her in the long, sleek black gown and white pearls around her neck, the elegant, beautiful young chick. I expected her to be polished and classy and all I'd have to do is start a promotion thing because I already had the contacts and friends in Vegas and wherever, and I'd just drop Marilyn in the slots and watch the jackpot money roll out. Boy, did I have another thing coming.

"She got off the plane in a crummy T-shirt and a pair of ripped jeans. She seemed as young and unpolished as Linda was the day I'd met her in a bar in Florida. Sure she was beautiful, but so what? Where was that gown and the pearls? Old jeans, a T-shirt, sandals, and two unmatching bags. I thought, oh, shit, we're back where we started."

Chuck had expected Elizabeth Taylor or the queen of England, with a thousand hatboxes and servants and rose petals strewn before my feet. "When I saw her, I realized I'd fallen for my own game," he admits. "Here was a girl I'd thought was a polished superstar. Why did I think that? Because of her publicity and the public image that had been created of her. To the public, Linda Lovelace was a polished superstar, but in reality, she was a mess. I was part of the public, too, in the sense that I had developed that mental picture of Marilyn and I had fallen for it. I thought it was going to be easy to work for a real polished, beautiful superstar, to work for everything I had wanted Linda to be. And then I saw Marilyn and I figured I had another mess on my hands. It all fell in on me. I had made calls the week before she arrived, setting things up for her in Vegas, Tahoe, Miami, because I knew Linda was breaking all her contracts, and the vacancy sign was being unveiled.

"Marilyn and I had good vibes, and that was important because otherwise I would have told her to get back on the plane and spend the rest of her life with that mechanic. See, good vibes don't make a superstar, unfortunately. We had to begin from scratch. All we had was a gimmick, this time Ivory Snow as opposed to deep throat, but we had things to do, singing lessons, dance lessons, acting classes, hairstyles to choose, dresses to be designed, arrangements to be written. I wanted people to recognize Marilyn every time she stepped out of the house. Who'd recognize her in jeans and a T-shirts?

"She was headstrong and tough. I liked that, I admit. It proved she knew what the hell she was doing. She was smart. She brought her attorney down and I suddenly felt she was a real women's libber, really dominant, but that wasn't true at all—but living with Doug was enough to turn any girl into the dominant figure. She was almost forced into that role of being overly protective of herself. No one had ever taken care of her. She had taken care of herself and her husband."

Chuck understood what Doug was all about, he was very perceptive. He showed me that Doug was a product of his childhood. You see, Doug's parents split up when he was quite young, and Doug did all the cooking and cleaning and the chores around the house while his mother worked. He took care of his brothers and sisters. He was a housewife when he was ten, and I don't mean that in a sarcastic way. It was the only kind of life he knew, how to stay home and keep the house clean while someone else went out and brought in the money. First his mother, then me. That's the kind of woman he needs, will always need. But I couldn't do that anymore.

Chuck popped my dreams of Vegas stardom within the next three weeks very quickly. "Marilyn," he said, "you have to understand we can't jump into this. I figure we have a lot of work to do and it will take time to do it. I don't want to have you get up on a stage till you're totally ready for it."

I thought I was ready already!

"What could I do?" Chuck says now. "I didn't want to hurt her feelings because her head was in the clouds and I just sat there and said yeah, yeah, yeah to her dreams, and in my mind I translated them into time and work and effort and energy. I had my calculator going, figuring it all out. I was sure it would take three years of hard work, intensive work. I had to be that twenty-four-hours-a-day thing, or not at all. Slowly Marilyn began to understand...."

And as I began to understand that becoming a real star takes a lot of time and a lot of work, I came to understand that there was little hope for my marriage. If I was going to be running around the world with Chuck, where was Doug's place? If I was in rehearsal all day and did a show at night, when would I have time for Doug? "See you next year, Douglas, and here's the rent check...." That would never work. I knew I couldn't expect him to accept my being with Chuck all the time (though I think he would have), and I couldn't accept it either. It wasn't right, wasn't fair to either of us.

And none of this had to do with sex! Chuck and I hadn't touched each other, our relationship was a business one. But that business relationship is hard to assess because we were feeling closer than we'd ever felt to anyone, in a "best friend" sense. Chuck was more than a manager, he was part of me, the only best friend I'd ever had in my life. I'd never had one, I realized, till I met him, and then I realized I had missed a kind of relationship everyone should have with someone at one time in their life. I could talk openly in front of Chuck, I could confide in him, cry on his shoulder, laugh with him, tell him my fears and my dreams, ask advice, be a bitch. It was wonderful. He understood me so! I could even talk to him about Doug and ask for advice on how to handle my fears about my marriage being finished. I really didn't know how to break that news to Doug, or even if I wanted to. Doug was so fragile. He depended on me. It was mother and son. I was keeping his cradle warm. And it's difficult for a mother and son to part. And, in the opposite way, I helped

Chuck get over Linda. I made his life less empty after she had left him.

In that first week, we lived a thousand weeks. We seemed to talk endlessly, and not only about Doug and our lives. The business of creating Marilyn Chambers was on Chuck's shoulders, and I had the job of becoming her. She was real, she existed in people's minds because of the films and Procter & Gamble, but she had to stay in their minds, and if she didn't go on to something else the public would forget her. Porno films can run just so long, and soap boxes don't stay on shelves forever. I didn't want any plastic images that I couldn't live up to and neither did Chuck. We had to concentrate on what was natural, what was me. That's what we would work at, that's what we would exploit. My natural talents, not another gimmick.

I think Chuck's right when he says superstars have to be consistent. Sammy Davis is the same Sammy Davis at home as he is on the stage or in the movies. He doesn't do a Jekyll and Hyde number when he shuts his front door. Burt Reynolds became famous with the *Cosmo* fold-out and everyone was turned on to how "free" and liberal he was, and then he came out with the statement about how straight he really was and his popularity faded rapidly. He's still around and he's a good actor, but he's not the celebrity he once was. There are beautiful Hollywood stars who say they're superstraight and in reality, they're balling every guy who comes down the block, or giving head to the kid who delivers their groceries. Or vice versa, the chick who's a starlet sex symbol and talks about her passionate love affairs, when in reality she's frigid. Jean Harlow was Jean Harlow all the time. God, she even died surrounded by the trappings of Jean Harlow satin pillowcases, silk sheets, and a canopy bed. Marilyn Chambers can't live in Walnut Creek, drive a '53 Chevy pickup truck, and be married to a bagpipe player. It wouldn't work. It might work for David Carradine, but he'll never be a Hollywood superstar. And he probably doesn't want to be. Ann-Margret will always Ann-Margret. The public thrives on them. Ann-Margret always looks sexy, and I imagine when she goes home she doesn't put on a sweatshirt and become a slob. I wear see-through tops and skimpy clothes all the time. I don't go home and crawl into an old flannel robe and turn into a frump.

Marilyn Briggs did the frump number. But she was a part of my old life. Chuck and I said farewell to her and we were happy to see her go.

It was strange that Chuck and I didn't feel physically attracted right off. That usually happens when people meet for the first time; they're attracted or they're not. If they're not, it doesn't happen later, it's over and done with. But it was the other way with us. Our attraction developed out of our friendship, out of our closeness, and I think that's a very secure way for it to happen. Of course, when I met Chuck I still thought I was in love with Doug and would be in love with him forever. I was still naive. Chuck and I didn't even spend a night together till I moved into his beach house in Malibu, and even then we didn't touch each other, even though we slept in the same bed. That was a trip, sleeping where Linda Lovelace had slept. Not the best thing for a restful night. But I'm getting ahead of myself....

Doug decided to come down for a visit. I'd been in Los Angeles about eight days, Chuck and I were very close, and we suddenly realized my husband was coming down and we both wondered, what are we going to do with him? He didn't fit into any of our plans, he didn't have anything to do with show business—I didn't need bagpipes backing me up. I was eating in restaurants, I didn't need to cook. God, but he seemed so out of place even before he arrived.

But arrive he did and he liked Chuck a lot. Wouldn't you know it? Doug was too nice! He was so cool, never suspicious that I'd be balling behind his back or anything. Okay, he had been great for me, someone to come home to and be with, never standing in my way, letting me do whatever I wanted to do, but there was no future for us now, I could see that. I didn't want to admit it but I could clearly see it. I saw that Doug was too trusting and too dependent on people. He'll be hurt often, I'm afraid. I only hope I didn't hurt him too badly. I don't think I did. We parted friends and he even said he was happy with the way things turned out.

Anyhow, he stayed with me for a few days, during which time we had no deep talks about the future or anything like that, and he decided to go back to San Francisco and get the car and drive down with some of my stuff. Eventually, he said, we'd get a house in L. A. and live in the way we'd been living. God.

Here's the part of the whole story I like best:

The people I was staying with had to move out of their apartment, so I had no place to go—except to Chuck's beach house in Malibu. He was the only person I really knew in Los Angeles. It was an exact replay of the way I'd begun living with Doug, having to find a place to crash when my friends left their apartment. Linda was gone and Chuck was my best friend and manager and we were together almost twenty-four hours a day anyway, so why not live in the same house, right? I called Doug in San Francisco and told him I had moved in with Chuck and he said great, Chuck was a nice guy.

So there I was, living in the house where the porno star I'd always wanted to meet had lived. Linda was gone but her things weren't. She had taken off like a gun and left everything behind. We didn't know what to do with all of it, if she would be back for her things or what, so I just pushed her dresses aside in the closet and hung up my jeans and T-shirt. Three weeks earlier, Linda Lovelace had been fucking with Chuck in that bed, and now Marilyn Chambers was going to be sleeping in it.

Sleeping is the word. But the truth was beginning to surface. I was starting to dig Chuck. I knew it and it bothered me because I didn't want our relationship to get all fucked up and because I was still married and I had never had another guy since I'd married Doug (the fucking in the porno films doesn't count!) and now suddenly I was finding myself attracted to another man and wanting to go to bed with him, and yet I couldn't bring myself to tell him that. As honest as we were with each other, that's the one thing I didn't dare say … or do. The temptation to reach to the other side of the bed and just touch him was overwhelming, not to mention the temptation to take his cock in my mouth and make love to him. I just curled up and hoped for sleep.

Oh, wow, I had a good hassle going on in my head those days. I had decided to tell Doug it was over but I hadn't had a chance to say that to Chuck; it was still brewing, I was forming the words or something. Then Chuck hit me with, "You won't be married to Doug for another six months."

That shocked me and I got uptight and, though it was exactly what I'd been thinking, I said he was wrong. I knew he was right but hearing it put into words made me start wondering if maybe getting a house in L. A. with Doug would work ... I was deluding myself. "Hollywood is Hollywood and Doug doesn't belong here," Chuck said. "In six months or less you'll be single."

It was fairly obvious to everyone—Sammy Davis later told me he could see it as clear as day—that Doug and I would split. Chuck says, "You can look at two people and you know you're going to take one of them and turn her in a completely different direction, and you see there's no place in that direction for the other. I couldn't tell Marilyn her husband was in the way of her life and future. I only told her it would end and let it come to her in her own time."

It came to me. I said, "Chuck, help! How am I going to do this?" But he told me I had to work it out on my own. I knew Doug better than anyone. Too bad, he really didn't know me.

I sat up all alone, all night, just before Doug returned to Los Angeles, watching the stars in the sky, listening to the surf hit the sands of Malibu. It was peaceful and so relaxing, it was what I needed. I knew I would tell Doug the truth as soon as he got to L. A. I also decided that once I'd done that I would tell Chuck that I was falling in love with him and that I was getting very frustrated sleeping in the same bed with him and not being able to touch.

But when Doug finally arrived, I didn't get to the subject for four days. I ran circles around it. I slept with Chuck and got hornier than ever the night before Doug arrived, and then I slept with Doug and it did nothing for me. And there were rehearsals, lessons, and plans to think about. Christ, what a time.

Doug moved into the beach house. He was just kind of "there," you know? I mean, there was nothing for him to do. So Chuck included him and talked with him and asked him to get involved in our business plans in some way or maybe build a garage onto the beach house—anything—because his life seemed so empty. He just sat around. He didn't seem too interested in anything. He pondered what he was going to do with his life, just as he'd been doing since long before I met him playing the bagpipes on that street corner.

It finally came to a head. Chuck was dating a girl at the time, Trish, and we all went out one night, Chuck and Trish, Doug and me, and our business manager and his wife, to one of those Hawaiian restaurants where they serve those knock-out-and-die rum things in coconut shells. We were sitting around a big table and the strangest sensations were going through my body. There was Douglas, and I didn't want to face him, and yet I wanted to scream at him that it was all over and he should go home already! There was Chuck, and the night before he had let his arm slip over to my side of the bed and I didn't know if he was asleep or not, but I moved closer and closer to him, until his fingers was resting inside my pussy, but we didn't talk about it because we both were pretending it had happened in our sleep, and I wanted to reach out and grab him and make love with him right there on the fucking Hawaiian table! And there was the ghost of Linda Lovelace, watching the whole thing, hanging over our heads. There was Trish, whom I was jealous of because she'd been making it with Chuck, and I wanted to tell her to take a walk too. And our business manager and his wife, they didn't fit in to anything....

So we all got zonked on pineapple floats or some such thing and when our food arrived, we could hardly see it. Poor Doug. He just collapsed. *Bam*, his head went down right into his rice and pea pods, and then he threw up on the floor, and again in the men's room while Chuck tried to hold him up. I was sliding under the table saying, "I'm really sorry." And I was. I felt sorry for him. It was the one time Doug wasn't cool.

When we got him home that night I said, "Doug, life is too fast here, too competitive for you. You either adapt to this crazy pace quickly or you don't adapt at all." He nodded his head and passed out.

So two nights later Trish came over and we were sitting around talking, Doug and Chuck and Trish and me, and it felt very heavy in there. We had been working on the act all day, and that had charged me up and yet taken away a lot of my energy. I was still jealous of Trish. Linda Lovelace vibes were reverberating in that house—hell, her clothes were still there! Her panties were still in the drawer! And Doug was smiling. Smiling! My passion for Chuck had still to be unleashed. I'm surprised the house didn't go up in smoke, not only because of my own feelings but Chuck's too—I found out later that he was as hot for me as I was for him and Doug was preventing him from telling me. So he resented Doug, but he cared about the guy too, he wanted to help him. And he cared about me but was a little ticked off with me because I hadn't yet told Doug the truth about our marriage.

So Chuck said, "I'm going to get some fried chicken." It was about ten o'clock at night and we were all hungry. So I said, before Trish could open her mouth, "I'm going with you."

That was the first time I had made it obvious to Doug who I'd rather be with.

I decided, while Chuck was ordering the Kentucky fried, that I would tell Doug that night, when we got back, after we ate the chicken, criss-cross my heart.

And I did, but I have to mention hypnosis here because that's how I got around to the subject of the future with Doug.

Hypnosis, you ask? Yes, Chuck had been into it very heavily, on a very positive level. He had used it on me to stop me from smoking just before Doug arrived in L. A., and in the past year we've used it in sex and it's great. We both have honorary degrees from the American Institute of Hypnosis. That's how Chuck taught Linda to give deep throat.

Anyway, after we'd finished the chicken I suddenly said, out of the air, "Chuck, are you going to hypnotize me tonight?" Chuck recoiled, wondering why in the hell I was asking that in front of Doug. That was the second obvious statement of my involvement with Chuck and my uninvolvement with Doug. I saw Doug's eyes flash back and forth and I knew I was finally getting through to him. Nice Doug was finally wondering what was going on.

Chuck and Trish left the room, thank them very much. And Doug said, "Does Chuck's hypnotizing you have anything to do with me? Don't you want to sleep with me tonight?" I said no to both questions and he shrugged.

Then I let it out. I told him exactly how I felt. I said we wouldn't be getting a house in L. A. and he said, "You mean we won't be living together in L. A.?" It took a while for it to sink in. "Right, Doug, there's no hope." He stared blankly. And then I felt like Wanda the Witch. I felt terrible. I told him it had nothing to do with Chuck, which was really true. I told him our lives had gone down separate paths and it was time to wave goodbye. I told him I was selfish and I had chosen a career over him, but that's what was and that's what we had to deal with. I told him that I knew he didn't really want to move to L. A., it wasn't his kind of place. I told him he didn't want to get involved in show business, that it wasn't the kind of life for him, that he'd be happier being a farmer in Oregon. And he agreed. He looked hurt and sad but he said he knew all that was true and he thanked me and said he felt free to go his own way. We held each other for a long time, for the last time. It had been easier than I'd expected.

The next day his attitude was even better. He said, "You know, I think this is the best thing that's ever happened to me." So it turned out for the best. It was good. It was bad, but it was good.

I've never seen Doug since. I guess I really did love him because I hope he misses me sometimes. That's selfish, I know, but then love is often selfish.

I never did go back to our house in San Francisco. I guess I believe that when you walk away from something, you just walk away from it. You don't hang on to knick-knacks and mementos, which will just make it more difficult for you. You keep the memories and forgot the furniture.

Apparently, Linda Lovelace didn't agree with that outlook. She came back, and we had her vibrators to contend with....

8

A Few Words from Chuck Traynor

I can't write this chapter myself for two reasons. One, I don't particularly turn on to the idea of writing the love story of Chuck and Linda. Second, and a better reason, Chuck can tell the story of his life much better than I can.

I think it's time you know his background, how he came to meet and marry the "deep throat" girl, how he lost her, and how, in his eyes, I fit into the life he'd carved for himself.

Go, Chuck, go:

Hey, my big chance, my own chapter! Marilyn's right, though, what she said earlier—that we're part of each other. Our lives aren't separate; they're part of one whole. But at one time, for a long time, each of us didn't know the other existed, and when we did know, for a long time we didn't care.

Where to start? The beginning I guess. If Marilyn will only leave me alone at her typewriter and get her hand out of my....

159

Okay, she's gone off to play with Sammy, our cat. So now, I can lock the door and tell all:

I have a Florida accent and I usually tell people, yeah, I was born and raised in Florida. For the record, that's only half true. I was born in New York and spent the early part of my life there, but we moved to Florida early enough so that I can't even remember the New York years.

The Brownie Shop. I gotta tell you about the Brownie Shop. I'm a brownie freak, I love chocolate. I have to endorse this product heavily! Marilyn and I flew from New York to Florida one afternoon just to eat those brownies for dessert, they were that good. "I'm a chocolate brownie, fly me."

When I was a kid, I had a paper route. Where did I spend all my hand-earned bread? The Brownie Shop. Charles—the main dude, the chef, the cook—and his wife have been there for twelve years when I walked in with Marilyn, and they looked exactly the same as I last remembered them. They didn't recognize me. I'm glad. Because they would have stuck me with a bill for about two hundred dollars. (Watch, two weeks after this book appears I'll get a goddamned bill for two hundred dollars!)

When I was a kid, besides being a paperboy I was a big show-off. And one of my best tricks was riding no-handed on my bike. Well, one day, going past the Brownie Shop, I fucked up. Crash! All of sudden I found myself flying through the huge plate-glass window, landing in a few cakes and brownies on display. I had planned on going in there, but not quite that way. I'd already swung my legs over the bar on the bike, no hands, and had my foot on the pedal, braking, stopping the bike, ready just to put my feet on the ground and walk into the store. So I came to a stop and fell through the fucking window.

I recovered faster than Charles or his wife did. I jumped up, in the middle of all that glass and frosting, and ran for my life! They never found out who it was, and I never dared go near there again. I used to have to pay off my pals to go down to the place and buy brownies for me. I remember I even walked by there with my parents and put a bag over my head or something. Come to think of it, they owe me a bicycle. They kept it, thinking I'd come back for it. But the bike was worth something like twelve bucks. The hell with it.

Marilyn started to say, when we were down there, "Remember the kid who broke...?" And I just pushed her out of the store with an idiotic smile.

Homestead, Florida, a rougher, tougher, smaller town you can't find. It hasn't changed a bit and neither have the people. When Marilyn and I were down there we ran around taking pictures of the houses I used to live in (or fuck chicks in, but I didn't tell her that) and all these people would come out on their porches and their fists would tighten and they'd stare at us and we'd get the hell out of there. "Haul ass, they're coming to get us." Hasn't changed a bit.

My parents were simple people, my mom was a nurse, just like Marilyn's, and she remarried and I really know my stepfather better than my dad. He ran a dairy and he was happy. Hell, at least we always had a good supply of milk in the house. And they were really very hip people for their time; they took all kinds of traumas in stride—well, most traumas. And I came up with a few for them. I have a brother, but he was the normal one. I gave my old man and old lady enough problems for both of us.

Like one time I shot myself through the leg. I really hadn't planned on doing it, like I wasn't trying to stay out of the army or anything like that. I skipped school (Marilyn and I have a hell of a lot in common, you see) and was out with my buddy, practicing "fast draw"! *Gunsmoke*, right? Well, I fucked up and pulled the trigger before I could get the damn gun outta the holster. Pow. Right through the leg. My mom wasn't working at the hospital that day and she knew what to do to stop the bleeding and get me there. I think she told me God was punishing me for not going to school or something like that. It didn't impress me much. I never cared for school.

I got arrested once for driving a car through a cabbage patch or something crazy like that. We had a sheriff, a deputy, and one police car. And everybody knew everybody in Homestead, so the sheriff knew all the kids and he usually knew which ones did which pranks. His name was George Right, which was a pretty funny name for a sheriff, I thought. He chased me many times, and if he didn't catch you, he didn't come looking for you the next day. There were no hard feelings. If you could outrun him, you won, that was it. If you didn't, he'd tan your hide. It was exactly like Bonnie and Clyde—if you crossed the state line, the law wasn't gonna bother chasing you, they figured the hell with you. "I'm not risking my ass in Oklahoma!" If you could outrun George Right and get into your own house, he wasn't gonna drive up and pull you out. Cool guy.

I was a badass kind of kid. I had a car before anybody else, the big shit, a real greaser-type. Black leather jacket. I dug ordering everybody around. Hell, somebody had to do it; otherwise, we all would have sat around watching the wind blow. So I did.

It was an unwritten law in Homestead that the rough guys played football. They were the strongest guys, right? So they had to be on the team. We'd have football practice and then a bunch of us would pile into my '37 Chevrolet, which I got in '54 I think, and drive out to some farmer's field and drink a case of beer and talk about balling chicks.

Balling chicks. The most important activity of my high school years.

I remember a high school story, much like the story of Marilyn's first fuck, because the incident happened on a rainy night. The night the lights went out in Georgia, man. I was going with this chick for a while and we used to get it on all the time, in the car, because we had no place else to go. One night we found out it was raining too much to park in the usual place, off this dirt road. Hell, it had turned to quicksand out there. So we didn't bother to go anywhere, we just stayed parked next to her house, in the gravel driveway.

So we were balling in the car and I thought I heard something. I looked outside the car and I see these wet footprints in the mud, leading up to the front door and back to the house. I thought, Oh, fuck, her old man, and he went back to get his shotgun. I said, "Quick, split," or something, and she's putting her clothes on and all of a sudden the car door opens and this big guy is standing there, staring down at me, and he says in a deep voice, "Come in here a minute, son." Son?

We followed him into the house and the chick stood over in the corner, thinking the old bastard was gonna beat the hell outta me. We'd been balling together for almost a year and a half and her parents knew who I was. Now, at that time a lot of kids were running off to Georgia and getting married. You know the South, kids get married at twelve years old, things like that.

"The missus and I, we thought it, and now we know," the girl's old man said.

I thought he meant our balling. So I nodded.

Then he says, "How long you two been hitched?"

Hitched? I recovered fast. I said, "Oh, … a few weeks." Shit, what else could I say? The chick just stood there, dumbfounded.

So the old man taps me on the shoulder and says, "No sense hiding things, son. I talked with the missus about it after I first seen ya in the car out there. You two can have our room for the night. We're gonna sleep in the parlor."

"Um, sure, great." I didn't know what the hell to say. He was offering us a goddamned bed—*his* bed—to ball in.

"Tomorrow we'll all talk with your parents," he said, taking off his boots, "and see how things are gonna work out. Have a good night, daughter." He kissed his daughter on the cheek. The father kissing the bride. Then he shook my hand and nearly pulled it out of its socket. And that was that.

Christ! I couldn't leave, then for sure I would get shot— deserting my wife? Hell no. So I did the smartest thing. I dragged the girl into her mother's and father's bedroom and we fucked till the sun came up.

So the next morning, we told them we were happily married even though we were living apart, but they wanted to meet my parents and get the big old happy family together. So we told my parents we were married. Nobody bothered to ask for dates or proof or anything. You just didn't lie about shit like that. We convinced them we wanted to live alone and they accepted it and it gave us free fucking time right in our own bedrooms. It was great. We kept it up for about a year and then we just let it die and I don't even remember what happened, maybe we told our parents we got a divorce, I don't know. I guess by that time nobody cared.

I used to have a motorcycle when I was in high school, and migrant laborers used to come into Homestead, and I started getting turned on to some chick who'd moved into one of the camps. I finally picked her up. Dynamite-looking, terrific body, long black hair (Marilyn says she doesn't want this in her book, but I'm forcing her to let me put it in—she says she wants truth, and this is the truth), I really wanted to fuck her.

She was wild, a freak before her time. She lived in an old battered shack of a house with her older sister, and her sister's husband or something, and we'd all go out and then I'd take her home because she had to be in by one. Her sister and her old man would drive in their old Rambler and we'd follow on my motorcycle. Shit, I can't remember the chick's name—Gonzela or something like that—but I do remember every time we rode she'd slip her hands down in my pants and start playing with my cock.

Anyhow, we'd get to the house and she'd go in and I'd say good night, and then I'd drive down the road a bit and wait for her. Man, she was sure crazy. She'd sneak out of the house wearing only a T-shirt, nothing else, and we'd go off in a field and fuck our brains out. Then I'd take her back about five in the morning, so she could get up with her sister and get breakfast ready and go out to the fields. I don't know when that chick got any sleep.

One day, or night, rather, she runs up to me and says, "I'm pregnant."

"Oh, fuck."

"I'm not kidding. I went to the doctor. I'm pregnant."

"Oh, fuck."

I was a senior in high school. I didn't want any goddamned kid. So I told my mom, "Hey, mom, Gonzela says she's pregnant."

"You're not marrying that Indian slut! That wetback! That pig!" My mom wasn't too hot on migrant farmworkers.

I thought, Oh, fuck, what am I gonna do?

"You're not bringing that Mexican bitch into this house!"

"Okay, mom, okay." So I went to my room and thought about the situation. I conjured up this plan. I gave Gonzela a hundred bucks or something and I told her to go to Texas and I'd be out there in three weeks.

She left

I never went.

And I never heard from her again. Which was fine by me. Watch, next week she'll call me and tell me to come to Texas and see my kid. Shit. I really don't think she was pregnant at all. A lot of those chicks would use that to get married, that's all. You had to believe them, I guess, when you were a dumb high school kid, but looking back on it I think she was happy to get the hundred bucks and get away from her sister. She's probably the wife of some rich oil baron in Texas today.

After high school, I joined the Marine Reserve, I guess because it seemed like the thing to do. I was gonna go to college but instead I went on a three-month thing with the

Marines. I think it was the hardest thing I've ever had to go through in my life. I was lucky 'cause I was in good shape from four years of football. But, man, they put you through fucking Parris Island and you hardly come out alive.

Three months was enough, more than enough of active training. I was glad I'd chosen the Reserves instead of that active-duty shit. So I entered the University of Miami and did my Reserve duty whenever I had to.

When I was in high school, one of the many jobs I had was being a loader for a crop-dusting company. I loaded big sacks of chemical dust onboard planes. And I got interested in planes and decided I'd get my private pilot's license. So I did. And I liked it so much I got my commercial license.

The guy I worked for the longest in high school, a guy named J. W. Holly, told me I could fly one of the crop planes if I checked out in a steerman. I told him I was checked out and he said, "Fine, take one up." So I took one up.

And crashed the fucking thing.

The landing was going perfect, but it got away from me as soon as the wheels touched ground. It slipped up on its back and I crawled out looking embarrassed as shit. And Mr. Holly fired me.

But a week later, he hired me back. God only knows what possessed him to do that, but I was glad. He told me if I worked off the damages (loading planes with that chemical shit) and fixed the plane myself, when I got it fixed I could fly it again. I figured that was great, so I worked for three months, hard-ass work, getting that plane put back together. Daylight to dark, working my ass off, never seeing a penny, just getting that wrecked plane back together so I could take it up a second time.

Steermen are open-cockpit biplanes. They're small planes that look like they just bolt together, but they're much more complex than that. The wings are wood covered with fabric, and I had to fix both collapsed wings, bend the wood and get the fabric glued down, all with the knowledge that as soon as it was together I would again take the chance of ripping it to shit. I really loved doing that though, putting that plane together, because it's an intricate kind of art form that we don't have anymore, it takes patience and precision. It's really like building a gigantic model airplane.

Well, I guess I thought I was Lindberg, 'cause I took it up a second time and crashed the shit out of it again.

Three months later, on the third flight, all went well.

I've always loved planes and loved flying. I crop dusted for about three years and then began flying as a copilot for a cargo company that airlifted live tropical fish out of South America to Chicago in a C-46, which will go down in history as the hairiest plane ever to make it through the clouds. We used to pray. That was the only way, the only chance we had in that big crate. I think the tropical fish even prayed. They knew they were in a flying coffin. In its heyday, it wasn't a bad plane but the one we had was the first off the assembly line, and that was back in the Middle Ages. Fire warning lights would go on over Tennessee and we'd go nuts trying to find out what was on fire, and it would turn out to be a short in the wires. None of the controls or gauges worked correctly, everything was off, like a clock that's always fast or slow. You're flying over the Gulf Stream in the middle of the night and this big orange light starts flashing. You're awake and you know what you're doing, but you're just not up to crash landing the damned ship on some deserted beach in Cuba or something.

I did that for about a year, and it was fine but the whole thing began to get to be a routine. You loaded the plane and unloaded it and fixed it and flew it and you got tired of it soon enough; you even got tired of tropical fish. So I got a crew cut (Marilyn's right, cutting your hair really does change you) and put on a white shirt and tie and became an executive pilot.

Now I was chief pilot for a big charter airline in Florida, and I was very young to be in that position, but I was very good and people trusted me. I ran a tight ship, as they say. I had a perfect record. I was proud of myself. But I was doing other things as well.

As a kid, I used to do a lot of skin diving, scuba diving, and I got interested in underwater photography. Now, one of the places I flew to with the charter company was a place called the Ocean Reef Club, and when the plane was empty I'd fly three, four, five hundred feet off the water and I could see down into the beautiful clear water, looking at the coral, the fish, all that great stuff. I think I was secretly looking for sunken treasure, a pirate ship filled with gold. Childhood fantasy, right? Marilyn had hers and I had mine.

On my days off, I got into diving down there, taking pictures underwater. I'd started doing that only because one day when I was a kid I saw a camera in the supermarket that was enclosed in plastic and would take pictures underwater. I probably tested it in the bathtub and got a shot of my crotch, but when it worked, I took it down into the ocean with me. By the time I was down at the Ocean Reef Club, I had a pretty damn good camera, I'd graduated from that $19.95 thing, and I was taking some damn good pictures.

I'd studied cinematography in college, never really having any serious intent of going into making films, but I played around with it and always liked it. One thing led to another and while I was still chief pilot for the charter line, I met Ivan Tors and worked for him part time. He asked if I wanted to work on a film, he was shooting in the Bahamas and I said sure. Being chief pilot had a good advantage—I could pretty much pick the hours I wanted to fly, so I was able to hold both jobs. And while I was working on the film, I met another guy who was a camera nut and he asked me if I'd be interested in making some extra money by going into "loops." Hard-core fuck films? Hard-core fuck films. Hell yes.

And they were selling like crazy at that time—I guess they still do today. It wasn't hard to find guys for them. Every guy I knew wanted to ball a chick on camera. We thought we'd have the problem of finding chicks who'd do it, but that turned out to be a joke too—the University of Miami was full of hot horny coeds who'd gladly ball and suck for a few bucks. They weren't kinky hard-core flicks like they are today, but they were pretty racy for their time, and we made good money off them.

So I bounced around doing three things in life—flying a charter plane, working on films that required underwater shooting, and shooting fuck films. I'd fly into Miami in the morning, work on the *Flipper* series in the afternoon, and catch a blonde sucking off a smiling dude on camera that same night. Hell, at least I wasn't bored.

(Loops have been mentioned in this book a few times, and I imagine some people don't really know what we're talking about. Loops is a word for an 8mm film, about two hundred feet in length, which runs about twelve or fourteen minutes. They're full of hard-core sex, no plot, no nothing. Jerk-off films for the privacy of your own home. They used to be shot in nothing but black and white, the kind of flick where the guy doesn't take his shoes and socks off and the chick wears a mask. But now they're getting very sophisticated, the color is good, the sex kinkier, super 8mm has been added, even videotape versions. But basically, they're your good old stag movies. The kind Linda started making.)

I was making a lot of bread as a pilot and I liked it, but I've always wanted to try other things in life, so I went into the bar business. On a whim, for the hell of it ... well, also because I figured I could make some bread at it. I took a regular beer bar and turned it into a topless/bottomless beer bar. Meaning it went from no profit to fantastic profit almost overnight.

It was in North Miami. I was still a pilot but I was getting away from it and starting to like running the bar more than flying charters. I always had a hassle going with the local cops, they'd try to close me down, but I never did anything illegal. I knew just how far to go and when to cover up the girls' pussies.

And that's about the time I met Linda Lovelace.

I'd owned the bar about a year and I had a big house, a three-story house, a tacky version of Hefner's mansion, which I lived in with three or four girls who worked for me. The Traynor Harem South. The chicks would run around the house nude all the time and guys would always be coming over—especially my brother—to check them out and walk around saying, "I don't fucking believe this." My brother hadn't visited me in years, and suddenly he was there every week. If you want friends fast, pass the word that naked girls are running around your house day and night. They'll be beating down the doors.

A friend of mine, Warren, needed a place to stay, and I let him move in and at the time I was dating a redheaded broad, Jan. Jan said she had a girlfriend who'd come down from New York and didn't know any guys. So I said, "Hey, a friend of mind just moved in, let's fix her up with him."

The girl from New York turned out to be Linda. We met at the bar. Well, she dated Warren and she'd come around the house now and then, as a lot of the girls would do, and we knew each other and it was no big thing. I'd been kinda looking at her, trying to decide which was the better-looking chick, the one I was going out with, Jan, or the one my buddy was dating, Linda.

One afternoon something happened and we started taking a shower together—Linda, Warren, and me and that's when I decided I really liked her better than Jan. We started rapping and she told me she'd rather be balling me than Warren so that was that. It was my house, right? Just like when you're a kid and you say, "You can't play soldiers here!" And the other kids ask why and you say, "'Cause it's my yard." Growl. Here I was, doing that when I was supposed to be grown up. Power, ah, power.

Warren didn't care anyway, he wasn't all that nuts about Linda, and there was an excess of chicks around so he didn't have to go through the trouble of finding another, all he had to do was reach out and grab one.

That's the time Linda was recovering from her bad automobile accident. She'd gone through the windshield of a car and was in Florida recuperating. Lots of people still ask why she's always clothed from the waist up in *Deep Throat*. It's because of the terrible deep scars on her stomach. They airbrush them out in most photos, but there are fuck books around, picture books, with stills from some of the loops she did and you can see them. I guess she's having a lot of them removed by plastic surgery now, but they'll never completely be gone 'cause they're too deep.

Before I met her, she had worked various jobs, in a boutique, a department store, as a waitress, nothing special. She was staying with her parents when I met her, very middle-class people, her mom's a waitress and her dad worked for an airline. She had a couple of sisters and I guess she figured living with them in Florida would be more pleasurable than New York while she was getting well.

I liked her and then I got to like her a lot. She grew on me. I was never really wildly in love with her. We just seemed to belong together. She was really sexually uptight. All she would do was fuck, the guy on top, a few moans, that was it. And I guess I was on a trip to teach her all kinds of new things. There was a kind of innocence about her that turned me on, if you can believe that. I dug her.

Her tits were kinda flat and she had had a kid when she was seventeen, but other than that I really kinda dug her. And I suppose the kid had been conceived in an innocent way, some dude didn't use a rubber when he fucked her (he was on top, of course) and she was too dumb to know. But I grooved on her, I really did.

I still had the bar and she started working there when she felt better. She danced and dropped her bra and showed her tits (but not her stomach) and we had a good time. We started living together, and running the bar and balling was really our whole way of life. I was making so much money off the bar I finally quit piloting a plane.

Then a friend of mine bought a place in Aspen, Colorado, and he wanted to know if I would come out there for a few months and put the bar together for him, to get it going. I knew the one in Miami could take care of itself so I said yes, and Linda was up for going to the mountains of Colorado, and she said yes too. We packed up, rented out the house in Miami, and started for Aspen.

In Arkansas, we got into a car wreck, totaled the car, wiped it out. We didn't know what to do. Buy a car (meaning spending most of the money we'd saved—we had been spending it like water in Florida and we didn't have all that much saved) and drive on to Aspen? Stay in Arkansas? Go back to Florida? We thought about it for a few days. I really didn't have a solid deal in Aspen, it wasn't in writing. I started wondering what would happen if we got there and the whole thing fell through.

Our answer was a drive-away car, just as it was Marilyn's answer when she split for California. The drive-away car was headed for New York, and it was a Ford LTD station wagon, which meant we could pile all our shit into it (we'd taken just about everything we owned 'cause we were planning on staying in Aspen for about six months), so I said, "Shit, great, we'll go to New York for a while and see what's happening." I figured we'd hang around and then get another car and drive back down to Florida.

So Linda and I loaded up the station wagon and took off for New York, with our cat, Hitler.

We had about two thousand bucks when we got to New York and we figured that would go pretty fast, so we thought about doing something to make some quick bread. I thought about flying again, or filming, and filming won out—I started shooting loops again because they made more money than anything else. And I started getting Linda involved, coaxing her into starring in them. We did a couple together and a few other companies (if you want to call them that) heard she was good, so they asked for her services, and pretty soon she became a hot property in the little world of fuck films. That's the time when she did the infamous dog films, which are still available in porno shops. She was one of the few chicks who'd do heavy bestiality flicks, so she was in demand.

Now, about that time, somewhere along the way, I ran into a company that was planning a feature, which would turn out to be *Deep Throat*. I talked to Gerry Damiano about Linda and told him how I'd used hypnosis on her to get her to suck just about any size dick in the world. He liked the idea, the gimmick of it, and I got to be production manager on the film, and Gerry and I became buddies.

Linda was my old lady and we did things together, balled together, and worked together. It was no big deal that she'd be doing a major fuck film as opposed to loops. There wasn't any jealousy at all. She was making money and we were happy and life was okay and interesting. It was a bit like Doug and Marilyn, only I was involved in Linda's work, pushing her into it, in fact, where Doug was the opposite, staying out of her way. But we were alike in the sense that seeing our old ladies balling some stud on screen didn't get us mad in the least. One difference, I think, was that Doug really was in love with Marilyn, but I never was really in love with Linda. After she'd hit, after she became a star, I was in love with the image of her being a personality, but I never really loved the chick underneath. That's the basic difference between my feelings for Linda and my feelings for Marilyn. I knew I loved Marilyn that week she started staying at the beach house in Malibu.

People ask about the deep-throat thing all the time, how did Linda learn it, and most people have heard that I taught her. I'd learned about it when I was in the Marines, in Japan. A buddy and I lived with two hookers who could do it better than you've seen Linda do it. It was crazy, one was able to let a guy put his fist down her throat (and up her cunt too). She could expand it and contract it and tighten it up like a clamp or a vise. It's a technique, and if you work at it, you can do it.

That's what Linda did. And she was good, though Marilyn can now do it better than Linda ever could. It's a psychological thing. Doctors using hypnosis usually say, "You don't feel a thing." I do the opposite; I say, "You do feel it, it really turns you on." I convince a person that what is happening is good and pleasurable—mentally. They can climax on that. And it can be very helpful.

Take a guy in his twenties who's been balling chicks since he was seventeen and he got hit in Vietnam and he's paralyzed from the waist down now and has no sexual feelings. With hypnosis, doctors feel that perhaps the area of sexual sensitivity can be moved to another portion of the body so these guys could actually enjoy sex again even though they can't feel anything in their cocks. They could feel it in their mind, which, really, is where you always feel it, ultimately. That's why deep-throat Linda reached a climax when she did it and so does Marilyn. The high feeling of orgasm is transferred to your throat.

People ask me if I could get them to perform deep throat, and sure, I can do that, but I don't play around with hypnosis. I mean I don't go around hypnotizing people I don't know. But what I would do is first establish total contact with the person. He or she would have to really believe in what I'm saying and really trust me. Now, of course, the first time is the time to go easy, and you lead up to what you want to accomplish ultimately. I use positive suggestions, telling the person how good he or she feels and how rested and possibly that something would taste good. I say "he" as well as "she" XXX a lot of gay guys have asked and written about performing deep throat on their lovers.

Anyway, I use my finger against their temple after the first time and say, "From now on when I touch your temple and tell you that you're going into a deep sleep then you will go into a deep sleep." It works. It's positive and it works. Then I reach a point with the person, just as I did with Marilyn when I first used hypnosis on her, where they want to do it, where they really desire to do it. That's why they're being hypnotized, because they want to learn this thing, and it becomes a simple matter of overcoming what is an involuntary muscle reaction in the larynx in the back of the throat. You know, when something touches it, you cough or choke. What I do is convince you that instead of coughing or choking when something touches it, you have a wonderful sensation, a physically wonderful sensation. You get turned on.

So I keep at it with the person and after four or five times, you progress to a point where not only do you get turned on, but you really climax. It works—it's the best fucking thing you've ever felt! And after four or five times it works by itself, without any hypnosis. I mean a person like Marilyn can achieve an orgasm in her throat just like the kind she can achieve in her vagina. Orgasms can happen anywhere, in your cunt, in your throat, in your ass. It's mental. With the hypnosis technique, your body doesn't react totally to the physical stimulus, but your brain controls your body. Your brain convinces your body that it's being stimulated.

Back to Linda:

Linda did a few more dog films before we started *Deep Throat*, and people find it hard to imagine that a girl whom I called "sexually uptight" at one time would find it easy to fuck with a collie on camera. I don't think that's hard to figure out at all. Most chicks are like Frankenstein. They are raised one way and they die. They turn eighteen and their sexuality goes no farther; they die, sexually, they freeze. But Doctor Frankenstein comes along and changes them completely, gives them a new sexuality and they turn into monsters! Good monsters! They go apeshit over sex. They go wild. They divebomb into it and never want to stop. That's what happened to Linda when she freed herself of any guilt. Untie that bondage and you unleash endless cocksucking. The Red Sea parts and so do the chick's legs. Linda did it all and more.

Linda loosened up to the point where every time she did the deep-throat number on a guy she came off his cock with a big smile on her face, the same smile the audiences saw and loved in the movie. That was her gimmick and it worked.

I never got uptight with Linda, off-screen-sex-wise, as I do with Marilyn. Linda would ball other guys and I wouldn't give a damn, or she'd let someone feel her up in a crowded hotel lobby and I thought it was a gas, things like that. With Marilyn, it's different. We're both very free sexually, but Marilyn's important and she is a star. We don't go to swinger's parties; it's like bringing a banquet to a sandwich. There's the beer and in walks the champagne. It doesn't make sense. But if we're getting it on with other people, it's cool. It's great, as long as it's our decision.

I do get uptight when someone tries to hold her hand or give her flowers with a note attached. I get a "he deserves a punch in the nose" attitude if someone wants to try to get his hands on her. Balling on screen is one thing, but balling in real life is another. It's private and selective and it's up to Marilyn to decide if she wants another guy or a chick, just as it's up to me to decide if maybe I want a three-way with Marilyn and some girl we know. It's not up to some punk to decide to walk up to her and grab her breast and tell her he wants to fuck her. That's happened a lot—she'll tell you those stories later.

Anyhow, we made *Deep Throat*, shot it in Florida on a budget of $28,000. It made $27 million. We made about $2,500 off it. Everyone shakes their heads at that, thinking we got royally fucked. Yeah, it hurts a little now to know the film made so many millions, but when it was being shot no one had any idea it was going to cause the revolution it did. It was just another porno flick, but a big one this time. What Linda got for doing that film was above standard. Twenty-five hundred dollars was astronomical for a chick to get for doing a fuck film. She was a nobody. Looking at it now, it seems unfair. But then it was fine.

Pornography is an art, and in any movie you're working on you hope for a hit. No matter what it is. You want it to be successful. So we felt that way about *Deep Throat*, hoping for it, but never expecting the explosion it caused.

We finished the film and the rest is history.

Linda and I came back to New York and then we went back to Florida for about six months, knocking around, doing nothing. Then we got a call from the company that had produced the film to come back to New York and sign a contract to do a sequel. A sequel? What the hell would they want that for? We hadn't been reading the New York and Los Angeles papers in Florida.

We didn't know that the film had become the most talked-about movie of the decade, and we also didn't know that there had been a lot of inquiries about Linda. *Playboy* and many other magazines were looking for her. We didn't know about any of it, we were lost in the swamps of Florida.

But the company had to find us, tell us what was happening, get us to New York, and offer us a deal so that they could get Linda to do the sequel. It sounded good and we signed the deal and then they sent us to California because the movie was taking over the town. Hefner invited us to a party at the Playboy Mansion West and that started Linda's short-lived but very exciting reign as the "in" star to invite to Hollywood parties.

We went back to Florida again, cleared up our affairs and involvements there, and then went on to New York to do *Deep Throat II*. The film was going to depend more on Linda's acting ability than her balling ability. Well, the film was a big flop. It doesn't take much to figure out which ability was the better one.

But I had a star, a big star, right in my hand, and I hustled Linda off to California to make all the dreams come true. I'd never really dreamed those dreams; they happened overnight. But they seemed so easily accessible, so within reach, there was no question as to what to do—go to Hollywood and storm the world! Hefner invited us back and said he would take care of all the arrangements; we shouldn't worry about a thing. He did, he took care of things, but he was a lot less excited about us the second time than he was the first time. Having Linda Lovelace around was a status symbol, but Hefner was a status symbol himself and he gets tired of people fast.

So we got a place of our own and right after that Pinnacle Books made Linda a fat offer to write her story. Everything was going beautifully. Linda's name was a household word from L. A. to Milwaukee to Tokyo. She was an international superstar. I was learning how to manage her, how to fit into the business, and one of the best things that happened was the Sammy Davis connection. I regret it now because Linda made him look like a fool, but at the time, it was the best thing that could have happened to her. Sammy had been a friend of mine for years. He was a big star. He got to know Linda and, partially as a favor to me and partially because he really liked her and believed she had some talent hidden away somewhere, he endorsed her. There were all kinds of pictures of them in the papers together, and rumors of them doing a stage play and a movie and whatnot.

Sammy and his wife and Linda and I went to Hawaii together and the papers played to up: SAMMY DAVIS/ LINDA LOVELACE OFF IN HAWAII! It was super publicity for her. And more offers came in, the biggest of which was the Vegas act, a complete nightclub act, which we planned to open in Florida and then take to Vegas. That's the publicity release Marilyn read and freaked out over. Linda was gonna get $25,000 a week. Not bad for a girl who couldn't sing or dance.

I should have followed Sammy's advice. He told me to hold off on it for a while and get Linda some training. But instead, I listened to my secretary, Delores Denton, who said that David Winters was "the" choreographer to have in Hollywood, and that he could work an act around Linda where it didn't matter if she couldn't even stand up on a stage. He could work magic. So I called him, hired him, and he went to work with Linda.

We gave David Winters $10,000 to start out with, to begin getting a show together around Linda. The first thing he did was to start bringing Linda a rose every day. Well, I should have punched him out right away, but I didn't. I thought, well, that's his way of pampering her. Pampering her, bullshit—he was deluding her. I knew she didn't have any talent and she knew it and he knew it. But he convinced her she was Ginger Rogers and Judy Garland and Barbra Streisand all wrapped into one.

I just never figured Linda would be so dumb as to listen to a guy like that. A choreographer, big deal. He knew how to dance and move people around on a stage while they were kicking their feet. I thought choreographers were a dime a dozen, just like hairdressers. They aren't managers, they're talented people who do one thing well, and the stars tell them all the gossip. And I figured most of them were gay anyway, but I would go pick the only straight one within miles, right? David was probably balling with Linda and I didn't even know it. I couldn't imagine Linda doing anything more than dancing with him, much less balling and listening to him fill her head with illusions of her great talents. She was dumber than I thought. And he was smarter than I thought. This stupid five-foot-four-inch dancer had a brain and he was stealing the biggest potential superstar in the country away from her husband and manager. (Yeah, Linda and I got married somewhere along the way, but I don't even like thinking about it now.)

One of the reasons I didn't see it was because I was really pushing hard. Career advances hit plateaus and they're hard to get off of. I wanted Linda to get off hers, in a hurry, 'cause it wasn't going to last forever. Linda was a lousy singer and a worse dancer and it was worrying me that she was going to get up in Vegas and pretend to be Connie Stevens. I didn't tell her that, of course, I mean I didn't put it so bluntly. I kept reminding her where she was at and how hard she had to work to make that stage act really something.

David, at that time, on the other hand, was convincing her she was terrific, there was nothing to really work for, she was that good, who needed practice? So I guess they balled all the time instead of rehearsing, I don't know for sure. I do know that one day, suddenly, with no advance warning of any kind, Linda left. Just like that. She just walked out, disappeared.

David's attorney called me about an hour later, protecting her, and his agent called and said that she was now going to be represented by him, all kinds of bullshit. They thought they had a goldmine on their hands. What they didn't know was she was a *potential* goldmine, one that had to be dug. You have to work hard before you find that reward. The mother lode is out there, but you have to crawl through the desert before you get to it.

Now, where I grew up, in the kind of environment I come from, when someone steals your wife you go shoot him. It's as simple as that. And I was very tempted to do that. I went up to David Winters' house one day and said, "Look, man, I want to know. Have you taken my old lady?" I didn't mean business-wise. I wanted to know if Linda wanted a divorce and if it was because of him. He told me it was a business thing and shut the door. I left without an argument.

Then this publicity statement was released that I threatened his life and that I'd had a gun in the car and all kinds of shit like that. I almost wish I had done those things. I don't deny that if I had caught the two of them together I'd have busted his ass. Our legal system doesn't allow that, but fuck our legal system in that case. I'm just that kind of guy, or I was then. Somebody steals your wife, you go get a big club and crack his head open. Fucking primitive thinking. I know, but that's the way I feel about that kind of thing.

And it hurt me. We had gotten married (oh, hell, it was somewhere between the two *Deep Throats*)! She was my wife! I never really loved her but we'd been together so long and our lives were so intertwined ... it really threw me. I knew the only way to recover was to dive right back in, to find someone to take Linda's place.

Marilyn.

People ask Marilyn if she's ever talked to Linda. She hasn't, but she listened in on a phone conversation I had with Linda the week before Doug arrived in L. A. All she heard was Linda's high-pitched voice screaming, "Well, fuck you, Chuck!" and she hung up. Marilyn, not Linda. Linda kept on yelling. Marilyn decided then and there that she never wanted to meet her.

I really didn't know that it was David at first. Linda just went. Poof. That was it. I sat down with Sammy Davis and we tried to figure it out. Why? Who? The "who" seemed to lead to the "why." He suggested David Winters and I said, "Him? He's just a short dancer. Him? Hell no." We went down a long list of names and the only one that seemed to make any sense, if you can use that word, was David Winters. David kept denying it, which pissed me off even more because I believe in a confrontation the truth should be told. It makes it a hell of a lot easier.

But I got over it. Really rather quickly, thanks to plunging back into work, thanks to Marilyn filling my life. I was happy the day Marilyn asked if she could move into Malibu with me for a while, 'cause it didn't seem the same, living there alone.

One night Marilyn and I came back to the beach house. This was after Doug had left for good, after Marilyn had told him their marriage was over, and Marilyn and I were making love by this time. We came back to the house and I went directly to the bathroom after tossing the keys on a table. Marilyn turned on the lights in the living room. Suddenly we both discovered that Linda had returned.

Marilyn looked around the living room, feeling strange. She didn't know why for a moment and then she noticed that the stereo was missing, the records, pictures off the wall, just about everything. And that night, before we had gone out, I'd said to Marilyn, "Listen, remind me to get the locks changed on this place. She might come back sometime and rip off everything in the house." I spoke too fucking late. Just about everything but the couch was gone.

I was in the bathroom and I wasn't looking around—who was to think anything was different? I said, "Marilyn, why don't you turn the stereo on?"

"There is no stereo," she said, entering the bathroom.

"Huh?"

"No stereo, no speakers, not tape player, no records, no tapes, no sheets, pillowcases, bedspreads..."

"Come on..."

"Linda El Sneako Lovelace had struck!"

Sure enough. She took everything she could get her hands on, except Marilyn's things; she didn't touch those. We went around checking every room, and the last one was the bathroom, and I'd already been in there and what could she have taken, the toilet? We looked in there anyway, and that's when we broke up:

Piled high in the bathtub, like a funeral pyre ready to be lighted, was Linda's collection of dildoes and vibrators. Her parting gesture, kind of an "I'm giving up this filthy business once and for all!" statement. A better phallic ending she could not have come up with. "Fuck you, Chuck. I'm going straight." She left her vibrators behind, off to seek a better world!

I don't know when Marilyn and I laughed so hard. At that point, we didn't even care about the shit she's ripped off. It didn't matter. We were free of Linda—the vibes were out of the house as soon as we tossed out her dildoes—and it was a damned good feeling.

I've often wondered if the garbagemen found them before they dumped the can in the truck and took them home to their old ladies.

Linda has done another book, which will probably be out before this one. I've seen advance sections of it (don't ask me how, I don't really know, all I know is I saw them) and it's very sad, because she's taking out her frustrations on everyone who once was close to her, who once believed in her and cared about her. Of course, I get most of the shit, but anyone with half a mind knows it's "sour grapes" and that kind of attitude isn't very valid.

I understand she accuses me of getting her into drugs, introducing her to dope, and forcing her into the drug culture. Hell, I never smoked a joint till I was twenty-six years old. I grew up on beer. As for hard-core drugs, shit, I don't know anything about them, I wouldn't know them if I saw them. Linda was arrested in Vegas for possession of cocaine and the charges were dropped because of the police's illegal entry. I was in New York with Marilyn and the nightclub act. I didn't have anything to do with Linda at the time. Her dildoes went into the trash and she was out of my life, period.

More than anything, I feel sorry for Linda. She's trying to paint an image of herself at anyone's expense. I guess there's nothing else left.

But life goes on. Marilyn and I have a lot of life left. The future looks wonderful. We're making it happen.

9

People I've Heard From— Wow!

I have reached people, many people. I've had hundreds of phone calls, but of course they're not recorded and I can't recall them word for word. Some have been threats on my life; some have been beautiful people telling me they love what I'm doing and what I stand for. Some are cranks wanting to jerk off and some are wrong numbers.

But the letters have been saved. I have file cabinets full of them, boxes of them, and I try to answer them all—at least the ones which are sincere. I think a good way to really get to know me and the effect "Marilyn Chambers" has had on people, in many diverse ways, is to show you a sampling of the letters I've received. They're important. Some are warm and tender, some crazy and wildly obscene. But they mean something, they fulfill a need in a person's life, and they do fulfill a need in mine. I like people, I like reaching out and touching people's lives, and I know I've done that by the letters I've received.

I really do think you'll find the following letters very interesting, and in some cases fascinating. And many of them are fun.

I've put them in here just the way they were written, with all the misspellings and errors, because they are human, and in a few cases pretty silly. And, of course, I've changed all the names to protect the people who wrote them.

You would expect me to receive obscene mail. You're right! I do, bundles of it. So let's start with the typical:

Hi baby,

What would it be like? Upon arrival of this letter I hope it finds you in the very best of health and spirit, as for myself, I'm doing as well as can be expected under these conditions you know. Let me introduce myself. My name is Barry Ainsworth, I'm twenty-six years old, born November 2, 1947, 5'10" in height, weigh 155 lbs., nice complexion, deep brown eyes and black hair. My nationality is Afro-American, a black man. I'm from Detroit, Michigan, but am presently incarcerated in Lucasville Prison. I'm writing you in regard to starting a correspondent course with you and making a new friend if I can find someone who I can exchange my ideas and views with. Let me tell you a little about myself and some of the things I like to do so you will have a pretty good understanding of me. I am a very liberal-minded person, very open minded about any matters almost. I'm a very aggressive person, I am very understanding and loyal and trustworthy and very affectionate. I love helping people if I can, I want the finest things out of life. I believe in free love, I love sex, as a matter of fact I am very oversexed, I like to speak what's on mind. I believe in satisfying a woman anyway I can in bed no matter what she wants to do in bed. I don't have no color hangups. I don't make no difference what color a woman is because a woman is a woman to me. Oh yeah, I seen your picture in the *Playboy* and you are really beautiful Miss Chambers, you might not believe this but when I went to bed that night after seeing your picture I had three wet dreams just thinking about your lovely body. I actually dreamed that I was really fucking you. It seemed so real too, you look like you can fuck baby. You know that was the first time I ever had three wet dreams in my life one after the other just thinking about a woman's body, so that tells me something. It tells me that you are the first and only woman who ever made me come like that in my sleep, I just can imagine how you could make me come if we were fucking for real you know. So I just had to write you to get to know you better and find out more about you. I think you and I have a lot in common and that is we both love to fuck. I would love to exchange ideals with you especially about sex, and maybe we could exchange pictures too. I have a few pictures of myself you know. You know if I was taking off sex with you, I would start off like this first with you. I would sit you down in my lap. Of course, my dick probably would already be hard. If it don't be hard when you first sit in my lap all you would have to do is just pull up your dress or skirt to your waist and just start grinding and rolling your ass in my lap and I promise you it will grow hard all the way to its full ten inches, then I would start kissing your lips until they get moist, after that I would start licking your lips with my tongue until you part them and when you part your lips I would stick my tongue in your mouth and we will just french kiss for a few minutes. Then I would take my tongue out of your mouth and kiss you on your forehead and then kiss you on the nose then kiss you on your lips again, and after that I would work my way around to your right ear and stick my tongue in and out of it until you start unzipping my pants and put your hand in my pants and pull out my penis and start stroking it and caressing it with your hand, and while you are still stroking this big black beautiful dick I will start undressing you and you probably will be undressing me too at the same time, and when I get all of your clothes off I'm going to start kissing and sucking on your breast until the tip of your nipples get hard and red as fire and when I see that I'm going to start kissing you all over your pretty white body, then I am going to lay you down on your back and crawl between your big pretty white thighs and spread your legs wide open and start kissing you on the insides of both of your thighs until you wrap your legs and thighs around my head and put that juicy pussy all in my face, then I am going to take my two fingers and spread your pussy open and then take my thumbs and insert them in the right place and pop that clit out and kiss it first, then start licking it gently with my tongue until you scream and beg me to stop, then after you come I am going to pick you up and carry you to the bedroom and lay you down on the bed and start kissing and licking you over every part of your soft white body until you come again, then here comes the best part, I'm going to turn you over on your stomach Marilyn and tell you to get up on your hands and knees in the dog position, then I'm going to tell you to reach between your legs behind you and feel how big and hard this beautiful black dick is, and when you get through stroking and playing with it I am going to take this big black dick and slide it between those white thighs of yours all the way in your pussy, then I am going to start fucking you slow and easy until it gets good to you and you start grinding and rolling that big beautiful ass of yours back, then when you start begging me to put all of this dick in you I am going to hold on to your pretty white ass with both of my hands and ram all of this dick up in your pussy and start long dicking you, I'm going to pump this big black dick in and out of that pussy of yours until you start ramming your ass back and forth with all your force, then after both of us come I am going to slide my dick out of your pussy slow, and then we are going to lay back on the bed and kiss and rest a little until you are ready to fuck again, but this time I will lay on my back and you will get on top of me and spread your legs and just ease your pussy down on my big beautiful dick and just start riding it like you are riding a horse. I think I have expressed my point in this letter Miss Marilyn Chambers so I hope you take this letter into deep consideration and reply back, could you send me some pictures of you, I would appreciate it. I hope this letter wasn't written in vain, I am very reversed on worldly matters.

Until my next wet dream,

Barry Ainsworth

I think Barry meant "versed on worldly matters," but we'll never know, will we?

For everyone who wants to act out their fantasies with me there is someone who wants to reform me, such as this special delivery letter I recently received:

Dear Marilyn Chambers,

I saw your film *The Resurrection of Eve* the other night, along with a girlfriend of mine, and I can't tell you how turned on I was by the scene before you enter the green door. Oh, I'm talking about *Behind the Green Door*, not the other film (it was a double bill). When I saw all those lovely chicks making love to you I thought to myself, She cannot be acting. She has to be liking it. And Marilyn, I firmly believe that is what comes out in your films, which doesn't come out in films other actresses have made, that you like what you're doing.

I guess I'll be honest with you. I'm a lesbian and though I sometimes like to play the "butch" role, I dress very womanly and hold a womanly job (secretary for a chauvinist pig, but I get paid a lot). I dig chicks a lot and I go to porno movies to see the girls in them, not the men. Well, seeing you was like seeing an angel, but an angel doing the real things we do here on earth.

Marilyn, I guess I've fallen in love with you a little. As I watched those women on the screen eating your beautiful pussy (thank God you didn't shave it like Linda Lovelace did for *Deep Throat!*) and sucking passionately on your lovely rounded breasts (your nipples are the most exquisite nipples I've ever seen on a chick), I reached over and started lifting the skirt of the girl who was with me. We had been out for a few drinks (it was our first date and had not yet been to bed with one another) and she let me slide my fingers up between her warm thighs and tickle her pussy through her panties. Maureen (that is her name) moaned a little and then giggled and her giggle sounded like yours. We wanted that scene never to end because it got both of us so excited. We talked about it later and we wished we had brought a dildo to the theater so I could have fucked her as we watched you being loved by those women.

Each time I saw a girl go down between your legs I would poke my finger up into Maureen's snatch and then, finally, I ripped through her sheer panties and my finger slid right into her hot pussy. But what was strange about it, and I didn't tell her this, was that I was dreaming it was your *pussy* I was feeling! Yes! I really felt as though the person on the screen was sitting right there next to me. Oh, how I longed to put my head down between your legs—Marilyn, I know what your pussy smells like, damp and sweet, like flowers on a hillside in the spring, so delicate and fresh. I would bury my lips and teeth and tongue into you and my tongue would lash out and tickle your clitoris till you shook in spasms from the orgasm I would give you.

Maureen let me stuff three fingers up her pussy in the theater, and when we went home we made love (I used a dildo and fucked her hard, just like the black guy did to you in the film, but my dildo was white, but it was just as big as his prick) in front of a poster of *Behind the Green Door*, which I stole off the side of a bus on the corner of La Cienega Boulevard and Beverly in Los Angeles. People thought I was crazy (this was before I had seen your movies) but I had to have it for my bedroom because your face is so beautiful. It is so pure. Do you know what I mean? You look like the girls I see in the drugstore cosmetic department, or maybe some of the young mothers at the P. T. A. (I was married and my three children still live with me). You do not look like the girls who go to the lesbian bars. They all have pimples or crooked teeth or seem "used". You are fresh and *my dream* is to make love to you.

Marilyn, I've never written anything like this before in my life. I've written letters to my mother and a few letters (sexy) to my husband when he was off on business trips during the first few years of our marriage, but never anything like this. I guess I love you so much that I'm not afraid to put into words what I'm thinking. I feel a bit liberated for the first time since my divorce. And as I write this my breasts are touching the pad of paper because I'm naked and a fire is roaring in the fireplace and the kids are asleep and I am dreaming that you'll join me and we can smoke a joint and have a drink in front of the fire, just the two of us, nice and cozy, and then you will lie back on the floor and I'll caress you with my tongue and my nipples, running my big tits all over your body, until they press between your legs, and then you'll open your thighs wide and I'll open your pussy lips wide with my fingers and I'll open my mouth wide and then I'll put my head into heaven, your wonderful, beautiful, soft, and warm pussy.

Oh, Marilyn! I just slid my vibrator up my cunt and I turned it on and I'm dreaming that vibrator is *your* hand that's tickling the inside of my body, tickling my pussy. God, if only you could be here now, to sit on my face, to kneel above me and let me chew lightly on your beautiful pussy hair, or, Marilyn, you could even pee on me, I would do anything you would like, I would be your slave, even though I am usually dominant, for you I would do anything. You will always be my master, my beautiful loving young master, and I will be yours to command. I masturbate while staring into your eyes. I dream of you every night. I dream of washing your body with bubble bath, drying you off, watching you go to the bathroom and kneeling in front of the toilet to wipe your pussy for you so you don't have to trouble yourself, then carry you off to the living room, right here, in front of the fireplace, and strap my dildo to my waist and slide it lovingly up your beautiful pussy and fuck you till you screamed in pleasure. And then you could fuck me with it, if you wanted, even in my ass …. Marilyn, I'm yours!

I know you like men, but I also know you must like women too because I saw a glimmer in your eye when the girls were making love to you that I didn't see in other films where girls were being made love to by other girls. If you can dig it, I do want to meet you, and I live in Los Angeles, like you do, and I have big breasts and a nice hairy pussy and a firm body for my thirty-six years. I'll enclose a nude photo and my phone number and address. If nothing else, please send me a naked photo of you—autographed right over your lovely pussy! You would make me very happy.

I have to stop now because I'm bouncing up and down on the chair with the vibrator in my pussy and my tits are rock-hard and I want to lie down in front of the fire, on the soft carpet, and screw myself with the vibrator, pretending it is you with a dildo attached.

I love you, Marilyn!

Lois

P. S. Once I smeared grape jam all over another girl's tits, when I lived in Chicago, and I licked every bit off and she went crazy. My uncle was in advertising and he did that once for a publicity gimmick for a movie. So I tried it at home. I would like to spread your pussy lips and pour a jar of honey inside you, and then spend the whole night eating that sweet stuff out of your beautiful cunt! Would you like that?

Well, yes, I think I would like that! I told you I love fantasies and that certainly is a fantasy. I don't think I'll do it with Lois, but she gave me an idea and one of these days, I will have someone pour a little honey into my honey-pot and let them lick it out! That would be a turn-on!

I wanted to laugh this letter off at first as just another crack-pot sex letter, but I reread it and I really kinda liked the woman. I, of course, liked the fact that because of seeing my films and writing to me she had become more liberated. I think that's very healthy. And it's a gas that she was feeling up her girlfriend while they were sitting in a movie theater!

But what I turned on to the best was picturing her living room—it sounded almost exactly like mine. Chuck and I have made love on our soft carpet in front of the fireplace many times, and I know how exciting that can be. I really could dig getting it on with a girl like Lois. I like romantic settings and her living room sounded super! And I think it would be great to have a girl fuck me with a dildo strapped to her. I remember how exciting it was when Helen first slid a vibrator into my pussy. Not only because it was the first time I felt a vibrator, but also because *she* was doing it, another *woman* was entering me! Not a man. Yes, a night with Lois could turn out to be fine, but I think maybe she's too much "in love" with me (the way people fall "in love" with movie stars and make them idols) for her to handle it. I sent her the picture she asked for and I know it pleased her. But now and then, I find myself thinking, what would it have been like to go there for a night? I giggle and I tell Chuck what I'm thinking and he jokes and says, "Well, we both shoulda gone!"

"But she doesn't like men," I tell him.

"Hell, at least I could watch!" he says.

There are people who want to be friendly and feel that in me they have made a new friend:

Hi Marilyn,

We are the couple who live in Elmira, New York.

Thank you for sending us a picture, it was so nice of you. You are a *doll.*

We saw your ad in our N.Y.C. book that we get here and that gave us a chance to write to you again. Hope it's okay with you. Hope everything is going good for you and we wish you all the luck in the world.

Marilyn, if you ever get around this area or get time off we'd love to have you visit us. We surely would show you a good time around this New York area. Okay! As you know, we work for a large appliance company and am sending you our advertising pen. Will you let us know where you will be going from the Riverboat so we can write to you again? Do you have another picture that you can send to us? Hope so.

Will close for now and hope to hear from you real soon. Good luck to you always.

Two special friends,

Brenda and Roy

P.S. Please write and send another picture. You're so nice and *oh! Yes!* Beautiful.

Brenda and Roy have written several times since then, and hopefully one day, I will be able to visit them. They're nice people.

Are you ready for more obscenity?

Dear Marilyn Chambers;

First I want to congratulate you on your sexy porno movies that you have been in. I really enjoyed supersexy *Green Door* with all those wonderfully erotic sex acts that you did.

I recently bought the April issue of *Playboy* and my favorite part of course are those sexy eleven pictures of you baby and I'm going to tell you baby on each picture why I love it.

First of all your sexy first picture and I love your sexy legs and facial expression. The second picture was great but it would have been better if it was bigger. And your third sexy picture is just plain sexy with your nude body lying still. I really got off on that one. My cock got hard just looking at it and rubbing my hand over your body, pretending you were right there with me. And your fourth sexy picture is very erotic because you're taking your lusty clothes off and showing off your sexy tight ass.

I really got off over your fifth sexy picture with your supersexy tight ass appearing like a big apple.

I'd like to take a healthy bite of that apple, and I'd like to spread your ass and shove my cock in it. I know you'd love it too. Your ass was really made for fucking, Marilyn, and I've got nine inches of hard cock that would make it wiggle and beg for more.

And your sexy, sexy sixth picture with your sexy body with you playing with your body. I'd like to play with your body and stick my fingers up your cunt and suck on your nipples. And your sexy seventh picture was really a sexy baby as you were taking a bath exposing your fucking good luscious body. I'd like to take a bath with you and watch your tits floating on the water. And your sexy eighth picture was also erotic because you were taking a bath and playing with your sexy cunt in the warm water, shoving my wet prick into your sexy cunt.

And my favorite picture was the ninth picture with you taking a bath and playing with your sexy body. I love this picture because you had a very sexy facial expression and a dreamy look on your sexy face. I dream about french kissing your sexy mouth. I love your sexy arms in this erotic picture and I wish they were wrapped around my body. I really got sexually excited looking at your supersexy breasts and sexy suckable nipples. My lips would fit nicely over those nipples and I'd suck them until they got hard.

And of course the rest of your sexy body is just plain delicious and your very sexy tenth picture with you taking a very sexy bath and loving every minute of it. You'd love it even more if I was there with you, playing with your sexy body while you sucked on my cock. And your sexy eleventh picture in sexy looking and great to watch your fucking good ass in action. And remember this sexy, my favorite sexpot is you, sexy.

Sincerely yours,

Your lover, Les Moyer

Do you get the feeling he thinks I'm sexy?

Marilyn:

This is your Master speaking. I have seen your films and I am ordering you to report directly to me on the first Monday in October so you can tell me why you knelt there and sucked off two cocks on those swings when they weren't as big as mine put together. I have the biggest fucking dick in the whole world. It is fifteen inches hard and so thick you can't get two hands around it. I am your Master my cock is your Master, and you will be my slave.

When you report to me you will knock three times and say, "This is your slave girl, Master," at which time I will open the door. You'll recognize me. I will be dressed in black leather, with my enormous dick hanging nearly to the floor. Upon entering, you will fall to your knees and take my member in your mouth and suck it till it gets fully erect. Then I will order you to hold your hands behind your back while I cock-whip you till tears form in your eyes. Then I will turn around and you will press your tear-stained face into my hot, hairy, sweaty asshole and you will suck it and suck it and I will feel your tears on my asshole and then I will spread my legs and you will see my cock hanging down there under my balls and you will suck it some more.

Then, my slave girl, you will be stripped of your clothing and I will tie you to my rack where I will insert various objects of pleasure into your cunt—a golf club, a broom handle, a rope, which I will pull from you fast, after it has coiled up inside you, and then my toes and my foot. Yes, I will bet you have never been foot-fucked before. You will, and you will cry out in love for me, your Master.

Then I will stand above you on the rack and strip myself of all my leather, except for the cock ring which I wear which keeps me erect longer and turns my organ a dark purple. I will stoop down and slap my wet cock on your tits and make them red with welts. Then I will stand up and hold my cock in both hands and aim it at your pussy. And then you will feel the sensation of a lifetime. I will take a piss on you, Marilyn, and it will hit your burning cunt and you will cry out and plead for more as the hot tingling sensation of my hot stream hits those thick cunt lips of yours. You will say, "Master, fuck me, fuck me with your piss as a lubricant!"

Then I will mount you. I will untie you, for you will be under my power by this time. I will mount you and ride you, from behind, slamming all of my enormous fifteen inches of hard dark cock up into your belly until you scream, "Master, fuck me hard, harder!" You will scream more than you screamed in your movie when that guy was fucking you. You will scream with delight because you will never have experienced anything better than my huge, gigantic cock. You will worship my cock after I come in your pussy, you will suck it and lick it and clean it all off with your tongue. And then you will get me hard again and jerk me off, onto the tile floor. And when I come all over the floor, in enormous spurts, you will roll around in my cum, getting your tits and belly and cut and ass all covered with my manly wet white slime. Then you will lick it off yourself as I watch you, with a whip in my hand in case you try anything funny.

You are my slave, Marilyn. I order you to report on the first Monday in October. I will be home after four in the afternoon. And after our first session, you will never cheat on me. You shall be whipped and chastized for fucking that black guy on the screen. My slaves do not screw spades. They are mine alone. You will obey and learn to love and adore me and my huge cock.

I'm going to come on this paper when I finish writing. And I am going to seal the envelope with my juicy jism. So you can smell it and lick it and rub it over your breasts, those hard tits which I will cock-slap.

You are my slave, Marilyn Chambers.

I am your Master!

Signed,

Your Master

This guy is too much! I've received four letters from him. He always knows when I'm doing a show and he knows where to write to me—Vegas, New York, wherever. Each time he sets a new deadline—October, January, April. At first, I wanted to tell him to shove his cock up his ass and kick him in the balls—or "stick your rehnquist up your blackmum and I'll kick you in the powells," as Gore Vidal might say.

The more I think about it, however, I feel sorry for this guy. I'll bet he's just an average businessman who is very lonely and has been dominated by people his entire life. I doubt that any of his letter is true—it is all fantasy, so he can jerk off while writing it (yes, he did, all over the last page, and it even arrived damp!) and get his kicks that way. And he must be lonely too. He seems desperate, and that's sad.

He's also desperate about his cock size. Why are men so hung (excuse the expression) up about that? I just don't understand it. They all think they're so small. Maybe because the guys in porno flicks are so big—but that's because it's fantasy, all women like to think we're getting screwed by the biggest dick in the world; all men like to think their cock is huge. Well, fine, for fantasy, but that doesn't mean you go home and commit suicide because your cock is smaller than Harry Reems' or Marc Stevens' ... right? I'll bet the guy who wrote this letter has a smaller than average cock and he's compensating for the insecurity it gives him by telling me how big it is.

Well, Master, I just hope one day you'll get it together. If S & M is your trip, fine, but don't use it as an escape—use it as something exciting, use it as an extension of yourself and your personality. Don't use it to create a self that isn't there to begin with!

Then there are guys who write me to try out a new comedy routine:

Marilyn,

For years I was a closet queen, but after I watched you in the *Resurrection of Eve* I got out of the closet! Now I'm just a queen. I really think you're a great girl. I would like to sleep with you, if you're not otherwise occupied. Please write me.

Sincerely and Devotedly yours,

Herman Catlett

Your majesty, I'm otherwise occupied!

I get some strange postcards, too. From hotels and Disneyland, places like that. And people write the craziest things on them. Here's a sampling:

Dear Marilyn,

My name is Jim and I'm a Marine and I saw your flick here on leave and I thought you are the most beautiful piece of ass I've ever seen. Man, would I like to put my equipment where your mouth is! When are you gonna do a live show like you do on the movie screen?

Love,

A Fan With A Big Hard-on

Now, I wouldn't doubt that guy had a big cock—a Marine? Aren't they all supposed to have big cocks? Well, that's what I was taught (and I won't tell you by whom). I read that postcard one night just before I went on at the Riverboat in New York and it got me all excited, I did the best show ever! I kept thinking of him putting his equipment where my mouth was. I even flashed that the microphone was his dick!

Dear Marilyn Chambers:

You filthy thing! I am spending this lousy eleven cents to tell you I hope the Lord takes pity on you one day. You are truly a menace to society. WE WILL RUN YOUR FILMS OUT OF OUR GOOD CITY IF IT IS THE LAST THING WE DO!

A Concerned Citizen and Mother

Marilynne…

Wow, baby, right on with that dude, Johnnie Keyes, right fucking on! Good seeing a honky chick making like that with a black stud dude. We're at the front of the bus now, honey, and George Wallace, he's driving, and you're fucking giving head all down the aisle! Right on, baaaaaaby!

SOCKO

Dear Miss Chambers:

I'm only sending this postal card in the hopes that you will have one moment to read it. I'm a twenty-one-year-old girl who was a virgin up until three weeks ago. I had always been afraid of sex, but I love Billy and he talked me into it. But it wasn't until last night, after we saw your film, that we were comfortable with each other in the nude. I think you did a wonderful thing doing movies like the one we saw. You helped me.

Sincerely,

Cynthia T.

Dear Marilyn Chambers,
Call 853-1212 for a *good time!*

That's all it said. I got the card when I was home in Beverly Hills, so I called the number just for the hell of it. Boy, did I feel like a sucker. That's the number you call for the *correct time.* "At the tone, the time will be…" God!

Dear Cocksucker Chambers,
FUCK YOU!
(You never answered my letter and you'll get yours someday!)

Unsigned

Hmmmm. I hope I *do* get mine someday! But not from him.

> *Dear Marilyn Chambers,*
>   I love you!
>
> *A Fan*

> *Dear Marilyn Chambers,*
>   I hate you!
>
> *A Fan*

> *Dear Miss Chambers,*
>   I read you're writing your autobiography—why don't you mention that you sent a picture autographed to me and that I have it up on my wall and I love it! Tell everyone *Bobby wants to fuck you!* I dare you!
>   Love,
>
> *Bobby R.*

Hey, everyone, Bobby wants to fuck me! (Hey, Bobby, does that satisfy you?)

I once got a letter that turned me on more than any other, but I can't find it. I've looked everywhere, here in Vegas, at home in Beverly Hills, even in a box of stuff I have stored at my parents' house. Someday I'll find it, but for now I can only tell you about it.

It was written by a guy who sent his picture along. He was very handsome, muscular. The picture was a Polaroid and he was sitting on the edge of a bed. The bed didn't have any sheets on it, just an old mattress. There was nothing in the room, not even drapes on the windows, the whole feeling was stark and drew attention to him. On the floor near his feet were his crumpled jeans and a glass of wine. He looked rugged, with a hairy chest and a thick, beautiful cock and absolutely huge balls. And he was staring right into the camera, as though he were looking right at me.

I remember staring at the picture before I read the letter—I couldn't take my eyes off him. I wondered who had taken the shot of him and then started fantasizing that I'd taken it!

Anyway, I sat down and read three typewritten pages of the most erotic writing I'd ever read. And he was literate, he was smart! But he had seen *Green Door* and was so turned on he had to write a "fan" letter. I think he said he worked in an office in Minneapolis but spent all his spare time on his small farm—I had visions of him walking around a little frame cottage, wearing just a lumberjack shirt, with his cock hanging out in the cool wind. I'll be that picture was taken in one of the rooms of his little house.

He told me he wasn't afraid to be honest with me, to tell me all kinds of kinky things, because he knew I wasn't going to answer and he also figured I wouldn't even read the letter, but he had to write it for himself, if for no other reason. He said he'd taken off all his clothes and was sitting at the typewriter pecking away while his pecker stood straight up in front of him. Little did he know I would not only read it, but I'd think about his letter often, and sometimes even remember it while I'd be masturbating!

I remember him saying he wanted to dress me up in a frilly 1890s dress and go for a picnic on his land, near a little brook. Then he said he would make love to me, lifting my petticoats in the air, nuzzling his face under them to get to my hot pussy. He wanted to eat me in the sunshine, under the blue skies, and he wanted me to suck him off as he knelt there on a little hillside overlooking green farmland and pine trees. It made me think of the movie *The Go-Between*, with Julie Christie and Alan Bates. It was exactly that kind of setting. He told me he wanted to watch me masturbate on his bed while he watched from his position, sitting on the windowsill, where he would be beating off. He said he wanted to cream between my tits and then lick his own jism off me. And he wanted to fuck me while driving his little tractor—he wanted me to sit on his cock and let it bounce up and down inside me as we road over the fields.

He told me he had a little dog who often licked his cock when he'd be going to bed and was horny, and even his asshole sometimes ... so he said he wanted to watch his little dog lick my pussy after he's filled it full of his come.

But it wasn't all kinky. Some of it was very loving and very warm. He told me how he'd been going with a girl for years and she was killed in a car accident and it took him a long time before he was able to see anyone else. He still belongs to her, it was clear, because he told me I reminded him a bit of her. He said he'd been in love, really in love with her, and he didn't think that could happen twice in a lifetime. (I wrote him back and told him, among other things, that I thought it could and that I really believed it would!) He said he missed the nights they would just lie in each other's arms, naked, playing with each other, she kissing his cock and balls, he licking her hard nipples, making love off and on, not caring about the world. He said he longed for days like that again, and when he saw my film and how much I resembled the girl he loved he suddenly had the great desire to whisk me off to the wilds of the Minnesota woods with him.

He told me that he was beating off while he was writing the letter—he'd type a paragraph and then pull on his big cock for a few minutes. And judging from the picture he sent, it must have been huge when hard, 'cause when it was soft it was big. I've always thought he'd be a knock-out in a magazine like *Playgirl* or *Viva* or one of those.

I remember the day I got his letter. I was living with Doug in Walnut Creek and I was bored. *Green Door* and opened only about two weeks before and there was nothing much to do when I wasn't promoting the film. The guy who wrote me had seen it in San Francisco and addressed the letter to me in care of the Mitchell brothers. He'd been in San Francisco on vacation and I almost wished he was there the day I read the letter and saw his picture. I told Doug about it and showed him the photo, but he didn't have much to say, as usual.

So I fantasized about him and once when Doug and I were making love, when he was fucking me very slowly, I started thinking of the guy who had written, and I dreamed it was his cock that was sliding in and out of me, and I dreamed I was dressed in that 1890s frilly buttons-and-bows dress and he was in his pants and suspenders and we were fucking right out on the grass in front of his farmhouse! It was a scene out of a Gothic novel, but a sexy one!

When Doug came and rolled over and started falling asleep I got up. He asked where I was going. I said, "I'm still horny, I think I'll go sit on the porch for a while and cool off."

"Want me to eat you?" he asked.

I could see he was sleepy. "No, silly, I said, "if I get *that* horny I'll masturbate!" I giggled and left the room. Then I went out into the living room and got some writing paper and a pen and the guy's letter and his picture and sat on the porch, writing him. I got so hot and excited I did masturbate, but I didn't tell the guy that in the letter. Actually, what I wrote him was very general, telling him how sincere his letter was and what a turn-on his picture was and how his letter really struck something in me, and that I wished him happiness. I wanted to write a lusty, sexy letter and tell him what I was doing out there on the porch, but I didn't.

Well, if he's reading this now he'll know the truth about the night I wrote to him!

I also get letters asking for advice. It was because of these that I started writing my column in *Genesis* magazine. For example:

Dear Miss Chambers,

I'm a young housewife and mother and my sex life has been a good one. However, there is one thing that seems to satisfy my husband more than anything else—a blow job. But the trouble is I can't do it very well! He comes, and he tells me it was fine, but I *know* deep down inside that he's had better. And I don't want to have him turning to some whore for a good blow job—I want to give it to him! We saw your movies and you seem to really know what you're doing. I'd be writing to Linda Lovelace, but Paul doesn't have an eleven-inch penis, just a nice average six, and I'm very happy with those six inches. I'm happy with the ways he fucks me. He's very good! But I can tell he's not happy with the way I blow him. He's tried to teach me to do better, but I just can't seem to get the hang of it. I recently overheard him talking to a buddy of his, about the best blow job he'd ever had in his life, when he was in the Merchant Marines, and how no one has been able to suck his cock as well to this date. Including me. I want to be as good as that girl, and I want to know some technique so I can please him the way he pleases me. I love Paul so much, and I would thank you forever if you could tell me what I'm doing wrong or right or maybe recommend a book on the subject, if there is such a thing.

Oh, yes, I also think you're a fine actress and from what I've read about you I know you're a sweet person.

Sincerely,

Mrs. Margaret Jacobs

I did write Margaret. I told her a little bit of what I thought was the right way to suck a cock, how to roll your lips around the ridge of the head, the most sensitive part, and to suck gently and let it work its way to the back of your throat, to relax and stop worrying if you're doing right or wrong. Just think of it as a big piece of candy that you love a lot, and go at it with that in mind. Lightly tickle his balls, play with his asshole, flick the head of his velvety cock with your tongue … all those things really help excite a guy. I know they sure excite Chuck! And they excited Doug, and the guys I did films with. Cocksucking isn't really an art, it's a state of mind, a giving of pleasure, and if you think of it more in those terms, the easier it will be for you to master it and become the best cocksucker in the world!

In the off-Broadway hit *Let My People Come* there's a wonderful song about "Georgina, Linda, and Marilyn." A fat girl sings about wanting to become a porno queen on the silver screen and it's very funny. But the truth is, I do get letters asking how to break into the "fuck film" world:

Dear Ms. Chambers,

I'm eighteen and considered beautiful by all the boys I've dated and I'm very pure-looking like you and I would give anything to become a star of dirty movies. I am very liberal and I don't care what my parents think. Can you set up an audition for me with someone who is making a big porno film? I would be grateful to you forever! Or if you would like to do a film with a costar, I would be honored to try out for the part. I have nice breasts and my pussy looks exactly like yours! Really!

Hoping to hear from you,

Sheryl

Or take this one:

Dearest Marilyn,

I'm thirty now, but I still look twenty-two. I'm a hung stud and I live in Missouri, but I'm willing (and able, got a great Chevy van) to come to New York or

Hollywood to do a film with you. I bet you want some new guys and cocks in your films, don't you? Man, you would really dig me. Could you maybe use your influence since you are the "top" in the business now and get me a job fucking on a camera? (And I think you are the best, Marilyn, and I can't wait to fuck you!)

Up and Coming,

Charlie

...fucking on a camera? I have visions of him balling some chick while they're balancing on top of a movie camera!

Some others are more to the point:

Dear Miss Chambers,

I'm better than you anyday—I have bigger tits and I can fuck like a rabbit and you'd better watch out, 'cause I'm coming to New York soon and I'll be a star and you'll be at the Riverboat still when I'm at the fucking *Palace!* It makes me mad seeing jerks like you up on the screen when beautiful talented girls like me are sitting in small towns doing nothing. You piss me off! So just be ready to start looking for a job at Woolworth's. I get outta beauty school in a month and then I head for the Big Apple.

A soon-to-be Star!

I haven't heard from her since. And I don't remember seeing her name in lights anywhere. Oh, well, maybe she flunked beauty school and had to do it all over again.

Jealousy is such a terrible thing.

One of the most heartwarming letters I've ever received was this:

Dear Marilyn Chambers,

I have been trying to make it as an actress for about five years. You don't know me or remember me, but we once auditioned for the same part at a theater in San Francisco. I think we both lost out. Anyway, I saw your film *Behind the Green Door* and I loved it— mainly because it was you. I remember how sweet you were at the audition and how determined you were to make a name for yourself one day. And now you have and I'm proud! I'm still working on the same thing for myself, and, like you, I'm determined that it will come. I think *Green Door* will be the "door opener" for so much more for you. God bless, and remember you have a fan who thinks you're terrific!

Marylou Mason

No, I don't remember her, but I'll never forget her letter.

Now, what about the people who are hoping I'm their ladder to success:

Marilyn Chambers,

I am interested in getting information on how to get into making stag movies. Where are they made and is it only in California or in the northern states? I would like to know what it pays for each one that you make. I have a nice-looking face, no hangups, and eight inches of cock that has never received any complaints. I like to get into all kinds of sex and I know I'd be good at it. If you can advise me on who to contact as I am interested in this kind of movies.

Thanks a lot,

Vince Fontana

I can't help you out, Vince, but keep looking, and maybe you'll have some luck.

Some of my thank-you letters are for other reasons:

Dear Marilyn Chambers:

We hope you will take the time to read this letter. We were not sure you'd be interested in hearing about us, but you seem to be such a warm real person, we are taking that chance. We're an average couple, married two years, and we were having problems. Our sex life was boring and starting to feel like a routine. Fucking was just plain fucking and then, to top it off, we have been trying for a baby for the last year with no success. Both my husband and I have been to the doctor, but they said nothing was wrong with either of us—maybe we were trying too hard. But I thought it could be because the excitement and passion was gone from our lives. We had lived together for a year before we married, and I thought it was always going to be like it was then. We fucked the same before as after marriage, but it was newer, so it seemed exciting. I realize now it wasn't exciting even then, just fresher.

Anyhow, we've been almost to the point of talking about divorce, 'cause even though we love each other, we felt if sex was dull, then soon the love would get dull too. Well, one night Fred was depressed and left house and ended up seeing your two movies. He came home so excited, but rather than tell me all about it, he said we were going back the next night. *And we did!* Marilyn, that was the best investment we ever made. You don't know but you're responsible for saving this marriage. We watched your movies, which, by the way, we really enjoyed and we both loved your acting and your sensitivity. But mainly, we left that theater knowing those movies had made a big change already.

We had great sex that night—relaxed, enjoying each other and trying new positions and new ways to satisfy each other. It was the greatest night we ever had in bed. We fucked and played for hours until we both were exhausted and started again right in the morning. Fucking had become fun for us again, better than ever. We've even told a few friends who were having problems and they went to see your movies. But here's the most exciting thing of all, Marilyn, I'm pregnant and you're the first one we're telling. Now I'm going to shout it to the world.

Fuckingly yours,

Carole and Fred Gardener

What a good feeling that gives me. I hope they have the cutest baby and name it after me—or Chuck if it's a boy.

Letters, I get letters. From every type of person, from every walk of life, from every level of education, and for every conceivable reason, I get letters:

Hi Hot Lips,

Marilyn honey, when I saw your pics in April *Playboy* I jacked five times before I noticed you were on more than one page! Honest, when I read a little about your career and your talents I decided to write and offer you a free (almost free) membership in my new club. It's called My Club. I'm doing ninety years, but I stand a chance of winning my freedom from prison, in a year or two on appeal. I'm an old porno hound and I've decided to be nothing but positive and successful for the rest of my life. I recently filed five lawsuits naming a number of attorneys and other pros as defendants. I've also decided to form my own club of fantastic broads. Nothing but the best. And while I'm in prison, it will be a pen-pal deal. Of course, if the members want to they can still belong after I get out. (Indicate whether just pen pal while in joint—or even after I get out—or undecided.)

First the rules, then I'll tell you why you were nominated for membership. 1. I'm president and the only male member. 2. President dictates all rules. 3. Female members must take oath; I, _____, swear to be loyal to the president of My Club, before all others, to always refer to him as mister or master, sir or big cock Daddy, and to always ask permission before I seek his advice, keep my mouth, cunt, and ass hot for him all the time, to use at least two fingers in my twat and three in my ass every time I think of him, to write him a nice hot letter declaring my love and desire for him at least once a week, tell him everything I do, and obey all rules of my big cock Daddy's club, My Club. 4. The dues change with each letter and will be described. First due, for each new member is—she must purchase a subscription to *Oui*, one to *Playboy*, one to *Penthouse*, and one featuring black girls, nude, in the name of the president. 5. Each member must think positive at all times—but if she's sad, she must write to the president giving details and then await his great advice. 6. Each member will not be jealous of her sister members, unless she realizes she wants her master all to herself. 7. Each member will seek out prospective new members and bear in mind that the president dictates the qualifications and approves membership. 8. Each member will at all times be prepared to war for her master, and ready to get down with a thorough fuck at his command, whether she is lucky enough to be favored by her big cock Daddy or whether he is still inconvenienced by prison. 9. All memberships will be suspended upon the release of the president from custody and each member will be offered the chance by letter to take the oath again and become a street member, in which case she must submit to savage rape job by her master in her mouth, cunt, and ass for one week to prove her qualifications and ability. 10. In the unlikely event a member breaks a rule, she must keep her cotton pickin' mouth shut about it or face the disapproval of the president. 11. President will change the rules as he sees fit. Any member not approving can complain to the president. She is obliged to expect a good ass chewing if she's that stupid. 12. Each member will immediately fight if she ever hears anyone say anything that implies that her master doesn't love her, appreciate her, or find her desirable. 13. Each member will learn how to spell "fuck." And do it often. 14. No member, even if she's hot enough to grill a steak, will ever accuse the president of making a tacky display of himself, or of being shallow, or moronic or creepy, or a lowly type. 15. The last rule now in effect is all sexy chicks who are nominated for membership are required to sit right down on their money makers and write an eager, long, passionate letter begging for the honor of being allowed to become a full-fledged member, which assures the president that they have already entered one subscription at least as a gift to the president. This will express their good faith and genuine desire for the president's cock, which, if he accepts said application, they can have anyway. It might help if the letter has a faint sound of desperate panting.

Well Marilyn lover, good luck in My Club. Now I'm going to tell you why you, Marilyn Chambers, have been nominated by me as a possible new member in my exclusive type club. Your hungry looking, hot lipped, hot hipped body for one thing. When I looked at your big nippled tits I got a hard-on in record time. When I turned the page and got a shot of your gaping ass, I came without even touching my tool. The pic of you kiddling your snatch in the tub got me ready again. And the last one where you are fingering your gorgeous ass made me fire again. The one where you got it turned up for a cock decided me you would make good membership material.

You sure are the best broad to hit Playboy in the last seventeen issues. Those other broads couldn't even serve to lick your cunt, baby, and couldn't do better than to suck your tits. Their big tits can't match yours for suck-ability—my mouth waters for you baby. Even in the pics where those girls spread their asses for a cock, they still can't beat your dick-hungry ass, baby. Yours looks like your president might get of lot of pleasure when you use it to milk his cock. Excuse me Marilyn love, I've got to jack again. See the occult article? Only two of them come close to you. The whore kissing the ass looks like she might serve to lick your leavings off the master's prick, but you no doubt could beat her by a full minute in a blow job contest. And the black bitch comes close to you, but you would still merit two cocks to her one.

I'm white, thirty-six, handsome, smart, strong. I used to just be friendly and dig chicks and I became addicted to porno between steady girlfriends. Turned down so many promotions I can't remember them all, and I ended up with ninety years. I've decided to change. I'm going to have a big club when I get out, but while I'm here, I think I'll limit it to fifteen or twenty broads. Nothing but the best will be admitted to membership, sweetheart.

Now you know both the rules and why you're lucky enough to be nominated. Before I sign off and whip this into the mail, so you can train your heart, cunt, and ass in this direction and get your money maker busy preparing your application.

But first (your first order, to be obeyed to the letter) all sweet-talkers are to be ignored when you are preparing your letters to me. Now, baby, I've thought of nothing but burying my stiff cock in your ass since I first saw it. You make me see you in motion. I dig your pics and close my eyes and there you are, taking pricks of all sizes and colors in every hole and in both hands.

Chance of a lifetime, bitch. You are very lucky. No fair asking how many members I've already got until you join. Quick, refer back to rule 15! I expect to hear from you soon.

Your big cock Daddy,

Richard Ford

    Big cock daddy. Wow, people really are into some crazy scenes.

My scene right now isn't so crazy. It's hectic, but it is full of love and good friends and excitement, the excitement of being a star and making a lot of money and performing for hundreds of people. Let me tell you where I'm at today....

And we'll save the rest of the letters for another book someday.

10

Marilyn Chambers Today

Chuck and I have been together for almost two years now and wonderful things have happened, my dreams have been coming true. The deep desire to be recognized for my talent has been realized by the reaction of many critics and the audience to my nightclub act. The desire to be called an actress has become reality; starring in plays and legitimate movies are no longer dreams. And writing a book, an unknown dream, came upon me suddenly when it was suggested that I tell my life story—and I've done it and I'm proud. Well, I have haven't quite done it—this isn't finished yet, is it?

I have so many little incidents floating around in my head, things I want to tell you. Things about the club act, playing Vegas, getting ready to do a major film, crazy things that have happened to Chuck and me on tour, what it was like to do all the talk shows, where the groupies hang out and what I do about them. I'll leave some of them—*most* of them?—for my next book. But there are some I can't resist telling you. Many are fun, wild things that have happened, many are serious and have a lot to do with where I'm at in life, but they're all meant to be shared with you:

Chuck and I often stay at the Hotel Warwick in New York City. The lobby is elegant and usually filled with people, and the staff is very efficient and helpful.

Maybe *too* helpful.

One day last year Chuck and I arrived in New York and the limousine took us to the Warwick and the bellhop took all our luggage and brought it near us as we were checking in. He stood by the pile of ten or twelve suitcases, at attention, ready to help us as soon as we were set to go up to our suite. Well, one of the most embarrassing moments of my life was soon to come....

Chuck was signing the register and suddenly the bellhop tapped my shoulder and said, "Miss Chambers! Miss Chambers!" I turned, wondering what the matter was. He was shaking and pointing at my overnight case, which was sitting on the top of all our suitcases. I didn't know what was happening—he was obviously very upset and people were beginning to gather, but I couldn't figure it out.

Chuck turned around and looked at the group of people standing around our luggage. Someone yelled, *"It's a bomb!"* And women screamed and everyone was afraid to go near our luggage.

"Oh, Christ," Chuck said.

I bit my lip. At the same moment, we both realized what had happened.

The manager came running up. "Miss Chambers, your luggage, something seems to be moving!"

My vibrators. I don't know how it happened but something set off both of them. Not one, but two. Inside the overnight case with all the usual junk I carry in there—cosmetics, toothbrush, aspirin, whatever—were my vibrators, six inches and eight inches respectively. And something had set them off and they were vibrating so fast and so hard that the entire case, which has a plastic tray in it, which rattled, like crazy, was jumping up and down, shaking. The woman who'd called it a bomb wasn't far off— that's what it looked like.

"Miss Chambers, what is it?"

"Miss Chambers, something is wrong...."

"Miss Chambers!"

People were shouting at me, wondering if I knew what it was all about, or worrying for my safety, thinking someone really could have put a bomb in the lousy thing. I turned seven shades of red and Chuck just lowered his head when I walked up to the suitcases—what else could I do?—and opened the overnight case and lifted two vibrating fake cocks into the air and clicked them off.

The lobby was silent. Gasps were heard and a few embarrassed chuckles, but talk about being embarrassed—I wanted to crawl under the rug. If it had been some tacky hotel on Eighth Avenue, I wouldn't have minded. But the Warwick! God! I don't remember walking to the elevator with the shocked and shaking bellhop. That was one time I really lost my cool.

And I guess it was one time I really lived up to the image of *Marilyn Chambers—Porno Queen!*

I'm often asked what it was like to get up on a nightclub stage for the first time—was I nervous and frightened and ready to jump out a window? The answer is I guess I was a bit nervous—I mean, that was it, folks, and there was no going back once you walked out on that stage.

But the hard time, the rough thing, was not the performance but the year of constant rehearsal before it. That's when I often wanted to run away and hide and hope they'd never find me. Every day choreographers, musical arrangers, my voice teacher, drama coach, Chuck, morning till night, working, pounding, sweating, all working toward that one night when I'd get up there and sing and dance. The test was making it through rehearsals. The opening show was almost a relief, I loved it so much. The night before the opening, Joe Cassini rehearsed us again and again, till six o'clock in the morning, making sure everything in the show was perfect. The stagehands weren't as professional as Joe was, so he worked parts of the act again and again till they came up to his level.

The opening night! Capitol Theater, Passaic, New Jersey, one of those big, old-time, old-fashioned theaters. A real stage, a marvelous orchestra, dressing rooms with huge mirrors and winding staircases—you expected to see the Phantom of the Opera flying around!

We started small, not wanting to let things go to our heads, the way it happened with Linda Lovelace. The Jersey show was a Minsky's Burlesque kind of thing, although my part in it was typical Vegas. It was a good way of breaking in the act and loosening up in front of an audience—which I found was easy, not hard at all, as I'd anticipated. I loved being up there, singing songs like "Light My Fire" and the old hit from the late '50s, "Green Door."

The reviews were good and the audience reaction was tremendous, but the most rewarding part of it was the experience I gained being in front of an audience for the first time. Thinking about it, and about the later engagements (at the Riverboat in New York City, a club), I realize I wasn't really nervous any of the times, and I don't get nervous today. I get excited, I become filled with energy, I'm ready to explode, and then when I go out there I'm ready to give them everything, ready to give my best. And that's the way it should be. The excitement is stimulating the way sex is, it's natural and a great high. I hate hearing how stars need pills and booze and God knows what before they can face an audience. Just knowing the audience is out there gets my body and mind stimulated. I have a kind of orgasm when I walk onto that stage for the first time each night. And you know I love orgasms.

In one of the clubs I played, there was a good-looking guy sitting in the first row and doing a lot of the songs to him really turned me on. And I could see by the lump in his pants that I was turning him on too. So, just as I was leaving the stage I flashed my pussy at him.

I think, but I'm not sure because there were flashbulbs blinding me, when I took my bows he flashed his cock at me!

That's one of the fringe benefits of having been a porno queen.

In my act I do a lot of head movements, when I'm singing, when I'm dancing, very much like Tina Turner, you know? Well, once I thought my wig was starting to slip, so I reached up and felt it and made sure it was on securely. I don't think the audience knew what I was doing, but Chuck sure did.

And, God, was he mad!

It's a no-no to touch your wig on stage, and I soon learned that. It's not professional. Can you see Ann-Margret adjusting her wig in the middle of a number? Never. So I learned, I grew as the act progressed, and Chuck was always there to tell me what I was doing wrong.

I just did a play in Vegas with Phil Ford and Jane Kean, *The Mind With the Dirty Man*. It was a wonderful experience but it made me appreciate nightclub performing all the more. In clubs, you have the opportunity to change your act every few weeks, or even every night, at least a little. Switch songs, do a different number to close the first half—you have the freedom to keep things fresh. In a play, it's the same exact thing every night. Broadway actors who land a three-year run must be superhuman—their job is to give an "opening night" performance every night of the year; the audience demands that and should get it because that's what they're paying for. Clubs at least give you some freedom.

Performing for me is a kind of sexual release—you remember I said I need sex more than anyone! Well, I get rid of a lot of sexual energy when I'm up on a stage—it's as though I'm fucking the audience. I have great fantasies still, just like I had fantasies about big black dicks when I was in high school. I dream the guy in the first row of the audience will walk up on stage and he'll let me fall to my knees with the spotlights on us and I'll pull his big beautiful dick out of his suit pants and work it hard with my hands till it stands up straight and tall and then I'll slide my lips down on it and make love to him that way. I make love to the audience as a whole when I'm performing; I'm saying, "Let me take you home with me!" And they're saying, "Yes, you can take me home!" I suck all their cocks when I'm singing; I rub all their hot dripping pussies. It's sex and I do it well and I love it. It is even better than the films because I'm real, I'm right there in front of them, and they know that and get off on it. It makes my pussy tingle and my breasts get hard as rocks when I pick up that mike and start singing to an audience. I only hope the audience feels it in their crotches—it's up to me to make contact with them and I try my best to do it.

The talk shows have been a trip. I went on the *Phil Donahue Show* (a terrific guy!) wearing a very pretty see-through blouse. Well, the producer freaked out. They said I couldn't wear that on the screen and I told them I didn't have anything else to wear. And besides, I like wearing sexy clothes. But I guess the TV screen wasn't ready for Marilyn Chambers' nipples.

So someone brought me a man's raincoat, one of those big heavy plastic things that guys wear in porno theaters when they want to jack off, and I had to do the show wearing that. I guess it turned out to be a good publicity gimmick because we received a deluge of mail on it, but it was so damned hot I felt as though I were sitting in a steam bath!

Phil Donahue is a kind of father figure; he's very gentle and intelligent and treats his guests kindly. People know that, that's why they watch his show. He never put me down for what I did, but he didn't understand everything either, which is cool. Of course, no talk-show host can endorse me they can only sound out my opinions. Otherwise, they'd get hate mail by the carloads.

Geraldo Rivera is my favorite of all, he's young and good-looking and hip to what's happening, and he's come to the closest to endorsing me. Or what I stand for. I really loved doing *Good Night, America*. I think it was my favorite talk-show appearance.

What question am I most asked on talk shows? Or by interviewers for papers and magazines? It's: What do your parents think? People are very interested in the family and what my family thinks of me, and I get tired of it. I understand it because we're a family-organized culture and everyone wants to know what mom and dad think of their little girl sucking cock on the screen. Big deal. They live with it, that's all. I get tired of having to talk about it. People should understand that you have to separate yourself from your family; you have your own life to lead. I think we tend to hang on to mama's apron strings till mama's in the grave.

The other question is: Did you really get turned on when you were making porno films? Well, if you've read this book you know the answer.

There are good interviews and bad interviews. An example of a really bad interview was the guy from my high school, some kid who'd wanted to date me for years and finally turned up in New York as a writer for *Crawdaddy* magazine and I gave him an interview, I was very happy to. It was pleasant. He kept calling me Marilyn *Briggs* and that was cool because that's how he knew me. But when the piece appeared I found out he'd never gotten over the fact that I had not dated him (all he really wanted to do was fuck me, that was clear) and he did a hatchet job on me as a kind of "sour grapes" attitude. I don't like things like that.

The Judy Bacharach thing was another interesting incident. She came up to review the show at the Riverboat Club. She's a very staunch women's libber, totally biased. She was very put off we wouldn't stop rehearsal for her, that we wouldn't take a break for her interview. I'm sorry, but the most important thing was the show, and she could wait. That's how I felt and still feel. She arrived at three o'clock in the afternoon and wanted to talk to me immediately, but we kept her waiting till six, only because we really needed to work on the show and she wasn't due until six o'clock anyway. We even turned away TV people that day—we had one rehearsal before the opening and that was it and no reporter was important.

Judy talked with me for an hour but I don't think she even stayed for the show. Maybe she hung around backstage for a few minutes after it started, but then she split. Judy did the interview with a chip on her shoulder, and in the interview, I told her the truth. I love men and depend on them, and that turned her off. Chuck was really mad at what she printed because she didn't give me a chance. She was so put off by my unfeminist views. She went so far as to call my outfit in the show "a pair of pajamas," when in reality it was quite a beautiful design by Boyd Clopton, who does Aretha Franklin and others. So I guess Judy Bacharach has Gimbel's taste in clothes. As she kept saying how much I looked like Linda Lovelace on stage. Bullshit! I look as much like Linda as I look like Martha Mitchell.

I hate alienating the press, but in Judy's case, I'm sorry, I have no control—neither does Chuck. The association with

Judy goes back to the Passaic show, when she showed up with some guy, who's a big promoter and wanted me to go to Philadelphia to do a show. He wanted me to go topless and show my pussy and get busted and with that kind of publicity he would sell out. Chuck told him to fuck off. If I show my breasts it's a tease, it's fun, not a gimmick to get the show busted. Chuck called her and told her that her newspaper was good only for cleaning dogshit or something. Oh, he's terrible, but she deserved it.

Women interviewers are harder than men because there's usually some kind of jealousy there—many of them are in their forties and they're ex-actresses or entertainers who haven't made it and they see in me what they wanted to be. It's hard because they're hard on me. The chicks like to talk to Chuck a lot more than to me because he has that charm and he doesn't put them uptight.

Male critics are less emotional than women and they're more open. Geraldo is hip to what I'm doing and he's successful in his own right, so he's not jealous or anything. I'm not a threat to him.

Talk shows aren't too different, and I enjoy them.

A funny thing happened at Nicky Blair's Restaurant on the Sunset Strip. Chuck had come in with Sammy Davis, Jr., and there are always a lot of celebrities in the place, so no one got all excited. All of a sudden, this chick jumped up from a nearby table, yelling, "Give me a pencil, give me a pencil!" Then she ran up to Sammy and said, "Oh, I want your autograph!" She was jumping around, making noise, and a waiter gave her a pen. Well, there was nothing for her to sign, no paper or anything, so she said, "Sign my ass!" and she bent over and lifted her skirt and pulled down her panties. Everyone was staring wide-eyed at his freaked-out chick and so Sammy signed her ass and went back to eating his dinner. It's amazing what fans will ask you to do! The guy who had been with the chick walked out and left her with the check.

Fans are amazing—and groupies are a whole other scene. I got this letter when I was at the Riverboat:

Dear Marilyn,

I will be at the Riverboat on April 27th, seated ring-side with a white carnation in my lapel. I am a young man past forty years of age and would like your company in my hotel room, where we can get better acquainted.

1) You will like me to stick my *big prick* in your *hairy cunt*.

2) My cock in your *mouth*, you will love to *suck* on my *dick*. Okay?

3) My cock in your cunt makes a nice juicy *scum bag*. I like it.

4) You will like when I suck on your shapely *big tits*. I love to *suck* on 'em.

5) Fucking feels so good. I love it, don't you? I will pay you fifty dollars for the trouble of *fucking* and *sucking* you all over. Do you agree?

We will have a good time. *Fucking feels so goooood! I love it!*

So until I see you on the 27th of April,

Your Pal,

Chico R.

PS: Fuck you! Love you!

My *pal?* Jesus! And sure enough, there he was, in the first seat at the Riverboat on the night of April 27. I made sure I didn't get too close to the edge of the stage for fear he'd reach up and slide his hand up my pussy or something! Of course I had no idea he'd be waiting for me outside, but there he was, with a limousine and all, standing there next to my own limousine when Chuck and I left the club. He was expecting me to run into his arms and go off with him and make that fifty dollars!

The guy with the white carnation. I'll never forget, when we started to get into our car, ignoring him, how he ran over and pounced on Chuck, yelling, "She's mine! She's going with me!" And Chuck and the other bodyguards quickly dragged him off and threw him into his own car. And that was that. But freaky incidents happen like that all the time.

Guys will come up to the house in Beverly Hills and knock on the door and my secretary will find them panting. Sometimes they just want an autograph, other times you have to call the police to get rid of them because they want to walk in and whack off in my bedroom or something! It's amazing.

Groupies are another thing, male and female. It seems the chicks get closer to me than the guys—I mean they know how to get through backstage security or something easier than the men do. Groupies are not all fifteen years old; they're all ages, from nine to ninety. I got a phone call from a young chick once who told me she'd seen the show and was disappointed. I asked why and she said, "Because you didn't take your clothes off." I thought, oh boy, all night....

So she asked if she could come up and meet me and talk 'cause she really liked me and identified with me. Hmmm. I said, "I'll call you back." And of course, I didn't.

It's difficult to be in a public position. It's the same old story—movie stars, politicians, rock musicians, famous writers. Whom do you fuck and how do you fuck them? On camera? Star-fucking is an interesting thing. People are into it, very into it—but the thing that most people don't know is that stars are into people-fucking! Chuck knows a lot of superstars in Hollywood and Vegas circles and they have a great feeling of power, which carries over into bed. Sex is a power trip. Superstar sex is an even bigger trip. There's the funny story of the Hollywood star who is adored by hundreds of thousands of women, all dreaming of balling him—and little do they know that all they have to do is ring his doorbell. Ding-dong. *Zap*—fucking on the living room floor.

Groupies give you crazy gifts—dildoes, vibrators, joy jells, things like that. I could open a sex-toy shop with all the gifts they've given me.

We run into stewardesses and travel agents all the time who are very straight people but they're ready to sacrifice their straightness for the chance to go to bed with a superstar. A stewardess who's never had another girl would make it with me purely because I'm famous. It's an interesting phenomenon, the power that goes with stardom, especially stardom connected with X-films.

It seems that chicks are into wearing bras again—especially in New York. Am I out of it? God, I think it looks ugly! But everywhere I go I think I'm being stared at because I'm the only one not wearing a bra. (But I love it.)

I recently did a centerfold for *Genesis* magazine, and was paid $26,000 for it, the highest amount ever paid for a layout, and *Genesis* gave me a big party in Vegas, at the Hilton, which was exciting and lots of fun. Being the highest-paid centerfold model in history makes me kinda tingle with pride!

Chuck has always told me, "Marilyn, when I die, I want you to have me cremated."

"Okay sure, Chuck…" My stock reaction. I don't like to dwell on death, I love living too much. It happens, that's all. But Chuck cracked me up when he added the following one day:

"And after you have me cremated I want you to douche with my ashes."

I couldn't believe he said it, I just laughed so hard. I guess I won't comment on it, I'll leave you think about it. But I'll say one thing—sex is a gas and Chuck knows it and even after he is gone I think he's gonna be getting it on, one way or another!

Me too—I hope.

I'm wildly happy. I have a marvelous old man, my animals, my beautiful house, my Jaguar XKE, I made about $300,000 last year, I'm playing Vegas, Tahoe, the best clubs in New York, soon I'm going to be in David Wilder's film *Arkansas Wipeout*, with Keenan Wynn, and I've been asked to do the film version of *Mind With the Dirty Man*, but now there is talk of doing it as a ninety-minute TV special, so I don't know what will happen. Everything looks so exciting. And there are all kinds of plans for the future—more films, a concert tour, television guest appearances, more. The best thing about it is that I'm the first porno star to really go legit. The dreams I had when I was a kid are all coming true, thanks to something called pornography, which is a good and wonderful thing, and it's too bad that so many people are uptight about it. Porno is terrific. Sex is terrific. Life is terrific.

Chuck and I have a marvelous $100,000 home in Beverly Hills. We fell in love with it and bought it because it was different, three stories built right into the side of a mountain, a pool which curves around the entire back of the house (where I can suntan in the nude!), a huge living room with cathedral beams that seem eerie and yet warm at night, especially when we have a fire roaring. But we haven't been able to spend much time there, almost no time there, because we're on the road so often.

And we've fallen in love with Lake Tahoe.

Yes, I'll always be involved in the Hollywood scene and the wonderful goings-on of Los Angeles, but the fact that we're there so seldom and the fact that when we're there the air always seems to be filled with smog—remember the days when I hated looking out the window my New York apartment and seeing the garbage floating around in the air?—make us wonder if it's the right place for us. Right now we're seriously considering giving up the house and taking our dog and cats and cars and getting a place in Tahoe, where the air is clean and the smell of green is all around and the snow falls in winter and smog is something foreign. Maybe. We haven't decided yet. It's hard to give up a house you always dreamed of owning one day. But perhaps by the time you're reading this we'll be living up there.

The house in Beverly Hills doesn't have a green door. But the one in Tahoe will, I promise! People ask if Chuck and I are going to get married. Sure. Of course not. Definitely. Never. The truth is, we don't know. Marriage isn't a big thing for us, and if we do it, it will be for very private reasons and it will be done in a very private way. Right now, we like the way we're living and have no desire to change it, but who knows how we'll feel next week? I love Chuck, love making him happy, love pleasing him, if that means cooking for him, singing a special song for him, or sucking his cock. And he loves me. That's good enough for now. Marriage? Even if we do get married, no big deal. We'll still love each other the same way we do now.

And does it really matter if I'm married? I don't think so. Mrs. Chuck Traynor or not, I'll always be Marilyn Chambers....

I'll always be your girl next door.

Afterword
by Valerie Gobos

Life takes us in many different directions, and for what reasons we usually do not know.

In April 2009, I got a call from author Richard Lindberg about Marilyn Chambers who passed away suddenly due to an unfortunate brain aneurism.

I was not familiar with Marilyn, but as we spoke I googled her and became intrigued.

I then called Seka who I know, and she told me that if I want to know more about Marilyn to call her best friend Peggy McGinn.

One thing led to another and Peggy invited me to visit her and her husband Darcy in Los Angeles to meet them, and a group of people who knew Marilyn.

I accepted the invitation and it was a fascinating day coordinated to talk to those who loved Marilyn, some worked with her, they told me stories about her, we looked at pictures, listened to audio tapes and watched videos.

I was getting to know Marilyn.

My final meeting was with Marilyn's daughter McKenna, who at the time was seventeen, and lost her mother and her best friend.

So, I became the chosen one to be sure that Marilyn's story is told and told correctly, because unfortunately she is no longer here to tell it.

From what I have learned in the past five years is that Marilyn was a beautiful, talented, sexy, strong, ambitious, smart, funny, intelligent, warm, loving and caring woman who wanted to be an actress, which would than lead her to success and fame.

She achieved her goal to be successful and famous, and before she passed she began to do mainstream acting as she had hoped for and always wanted to do.

She seemed happy and had no regrets for the path that she chose in her life. And she had a great time living it!

When she passed away quickly and quietly at too young of an age, she accomplished so much but she had more that she wanted to do.

As she stated many times, her biggest accomplishment of all was her beautiful daughter McKenna, who she referred to as the ' *love of her life* ' This has been a more than interesting journey for me, and I am privileged to be the one to ensure that Marilyn's story is told as she would have wanted it.

So stay tuned for more of Marilyn Chambers!

CPSIA information can be obtained
at www.ICGtesting.com
Printed in the USA
BVHW041031130619
550940BV00010B/349/P